THE ODD COUPLE

THE
ODD COUPLE

•

by

Neil Simon

Random House New York

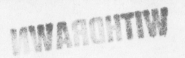

Photographs by courtesy of Friedman-Abeles

Library of Congress Catalog Card Number: 66-22251

MANUFACTURED IN THE UNITED STATES OF AMERICA

To *Danny* AND *Roy*

THE ODD COUPLE *was first presented by Saint Subber on March 10, 1965, at the Plymouth Theatre in New York City, with the following cast:*

(In order of appearance)

SPEED	Paul Dooley
MURRAY	Nathaniel Frey
ROY	Sidney Armus
VINNIE	John Fiedler
OSCAR MADISON	Walter Matthau
FELIX UNGAR	Art Carney
GWENDOLYN PIGEON	Carole Shelley
CECILY PIGEON	Monica Evans

Written by Neil Simon
Directed by Mike Nichols
Set designed by Oliver Smith
Lighting by Jean Rosenthal
Costumes by Ann Roth

Act One

It is a warm summer night in OSCAR MADISON's apartment. This is one of those large eight-room affairs on Riverside Drive in the upper eighties. The building is about thirty-five years old and still has vestiges of its glorious past —high ceilings, walk-in closets and thick walls. We are in the living room with doors leading off to the kitchen, a bedroom and a bathroom, and a hallway to the other bedrooms.

Although the furnishings have been chosen with extreme good taste, the room itself, without the touch and care of a woman these past few months, is now a study in slovenliness. Dirty dishes, discarded clothes, old newspapers, empty bottles, glasses filled and unfilled, opened and unopened laundry packages, mail and disarrayed furniture abound. The only cheerful note left in this room is the lovely view of the New Jersey Palisades through its twelfth-floor window. Three months ago this was a lovely apartment.

As the curtain rises, the room is filled with smoke. A poker game is in progress. There are six chairs around the table but only four men are sitting. They are MURRAY, ROY, SPEED and VINNIE. VINNIE, with the largest stack of chips in front of him, is nervously tapping his foot; he keeps checking his watch. ROY is watching SPEED and SPEED is

3

glaring at MURRAY *with incredulity and utter fascination.* MURRAY *is the dealer. He slowly and methodically tries to shuffle. It is a ponderous and painful business.* SPEED *shakes his head in disbelief. This is all done wordlessly.*

SPEED (*Cups his chin in his hand and looks at* MURRAY) Tell me, Mr. Maverick, is this your first time on the riverboat?

MURRAY (*With utter disregard*) You don't like it, get a machine.
(*He continues to deal slowly*)

ROY Geez, it stinks in here.

VINNIE (*Looks at his watch*) What time is it?

SPEED Again what time is it?

VINNIE (*Whining*) My watch is slow. I'd like to know what time it is.

SPEED (*Glares at him*) You're winning ninety-five dollars, that's what time it is. Where the hell are you running?

VINNIE I'm not running anywhere. I just asked what time it was. Who said anything about running?

ROY (*Looks at his watch*) It's ten-thirty.
(*There is a pause.* MURRAY *continues to shuffle*)

VINNIE (*After the pause*) I got to leave by twelve.

SPEED (*Looks up in despair*) Oh, Christ!

VINNIE I told you that when I sat down. I got to leave by twelve. Murray, didn't I say that when I sat down? I said I got to leave by twelve.

SPEED All right, don't talk to him. He's dealing. (*To* MURRAY) Murray, you wanna rest for a while? Go lie down, sweetheart.

MURRAY You want speed or accuracy, make up your mind.

(He begins to deal slowly. SPEED puffs on his cigar angrily)

ROY Hey, you want to do me a really big favor? Smoke toward New Jersey.

(SPEED blows smoke at ROY)

MURRAY No kidding, I'm really worried about Felix. *(Points to an empty chair)* He's never been this late before. Maybe somebody should call. *(Yells off)* Hey, Oscar, why don't you call Felix?

ROY *(Waves his hand through the smoke)* Listen, why don't we chip in three dollars apiece and buy another window. How the hell can you breathe in here?

MURRAY How many cards you got, four?

SPEED Yes, Murray, we all have four cards. When you give us one more, we'll all have five. If you were to give us two more, we'd have six. Understand how it works now?

ROY *(Yells off)* Hey, Oscar, what do you say? In or out?

(From offstage we hear OSCAR's voice)

OSCAR *(Offstage)* Out, pussycat, out!

(SPEED opens and the others bet)

VINNIE I told my wife I'd be home by one the latest. We're making an eight o'clock plane to Florida. I told you that when I sat down.

SPEED Don't cry, Vinnie. You're forty-two years old. It's embarrassing. Give me two . . .

(He discards)

ROY   Why doesn't he fix the air conditioner? It's ninety-eight degrees, and it sits there sweating like everyone else. I'm out.
  (*He goes to the window and looks out*)

MURRAY   Who goes to Florida in July?

VINNIE   It's off-season. There's no crowds and you get the best room for one-tenth the price. No cards . . .

SPEED   Some vacation. Six cheap people in an empty hotel.

MURRAY   Dealer takes four . . . Hey, you think maybe Felix is sick? (*He points to the empty chair*) I mean he's never been this late before.

ROY (*Takes a laundry bag from an armchair and sits*)   You know, it's the same garbage from last week's game. I'm beginning to recognize things.

MURRAY (*Throwing his cards down*)   I'm out . . .

SPEED (*Showing his hand*)   Two kings . . .

VINNIE   Straight . . .
  (*He shows his hand and takes in the pot*)

MURRAY   Hey, maybe he's in his office locked in the john again. Did you know Felix was once locked in the john overnight. He wrote out his entire will on a half a roll of toilet paper! Heee, what a nut!
  (VINNIE *is playing with his chips*)

SPEED (*Glares at him as he shuffles the cards*)   Don't play with your chips. I'm asking you nice; don't play with your chips.

VINNIE (*To* SPEED)   I'm not playing. I'm counting. Leave me alone. What are you picking on me for? How much do you think I'm winning? Fifteen dollars!

SPEED Fifteen dollars? You dropped more than that in your cuffs!

> (SPEED *deals a game of draw poker*)

MURRAY (*Yells off*) Hey, Oscar, what do you say?

OSCAR (*Enters carrying a tray with beer, sandwiches, a can of peanuts, and opened bags of pretzels and Fritos*) I'm in! I'm in! Go ahead. Deal!

> (OSCAR MADISON *is forty-three. He is a pleasant, appealing man who seems to enjoy life to the fullest. He enjoys his weekly poker game, his friends, his excessive drinking and his cigars. He is also one of those lucky creatures in life who even enjoys his work—he's a sports-writer for the New York Post. His carefree attitude is evident in the sloppiness of his household, but it seems to bother others more than it does* OSCAR. *This is not to say that* OSCAR *is without cares or worries. He just doesn't seem to have any*)

VINNIE Aren't you going to look at your cards?

OSCAR (*Sets the tray on a side chair*) What for? I'm gonna bluff anyway. (*Opens a bottle of Coke*) Who gets the Coke?

MURRAY I get a Coke.

OSCAR My friend Murray the policeman gets a warm Coke.

> (*He gives him the bottle*)

ROY (*Opens the betting*) You still didn't fix the refrigerator? It's been two weeks now. No wonder it stinks in here.

OSCAR (*Picks up his cards*) Temper, temper. If I wanted

7

nagging I'd go back with my wife. (*Throws them down*) I'm out. Who wants food?

MURRAY What have you got?

OSCAR (*Looks under the bread*) I got brown sandwiches and green sandwiches. Well, what do you say?

MURRAY What's the green?

OSCAR It's either very new cheese or very old meat.

MURRAY I'll take the brown.
    (OSCAR *gives* MURRAY *a sandwich*)

ROY (*Glares at* MURRAY) Are you crazy? You're not going to eat that, are you?

MURRAY I'm hungry.

ROY His refrigerator's been broken for two weeks. I saw milk standing in there that wasn't even in the bottle.

OSCAR (*To* ROY) What are you, some kind of a health nut? Eat, Murray, eat!

ROY I've got six cards . . .

SPEED That figures—I've got three aces. Misdeal.
    (*They all throw their cards in.* SPEED *begins to shuffle*)

VINNIE You know who makes very good sandwiches? Felix. Did you ever taste his cream cheese and pimento on date-nut bread?

SPEED (*To* VINNIE) All right, make up your mind: poker or menus. (OSCAR *opens a can of beer, which sprays in a geyser over the players and the table. There is a hubbub as they all yell at* OSCAR. *He hands* ROY *the overflowing can and pushes the puddle of beer under the chair. The players start to go back to the game only to be sprayed again as* OSCAR *opens another beer can. There is another outraged cry as they try to stop* OSCAR *and mop up the beer on the table with a towel which was hanging on the standing lamp.* OSCAR, *undisturbed, gives them the beer and the bags of refreshments, and they finally sit back in their chairs.* OSCAR *wipes his hands on the sleeve of* ROY's *jacket which is hanging on the back of the chair*) Hey, Vinnie, tell Oscar what time you're leaving.

VINNIE (*Like a trained dog*)   Twelve o'clock.

SPEED (*To the others*)   You hear? We got ten minutes before the next announcement. All right, this game is five card stud. (*He deals and ad libs calling the cards, ending with* MURRAY's *card*) . . . And a bullet for the policeman. All right, Murray, it's your bet. (*No answer*) Do something, huh.

OSCAR (*Getting a drink at the bar*)   Don't yell at my friend Murray.

MURRAY (*Throwing in a coin*)   I'm in for a quarter.

OSCAR (*Proudly looks in* MURRAY's *eyes*)   Beautiful, baby, beautiful.

> (*He sits down and begins to open the can of peanuts*)

ROY   Hey, Oscar, let's make a rule. Every six months you have to buy fresh potato chips. How can you live like this? Don't you have a maid?

OSCAR (*Shakes his head*)   She quit after my wife and kids left. The work got to be too much for her. (*He looks on the table*) The pot's shy. Who didn't put in a quarter?

MURRAY (*To* OSCAR)   You didn't.

OSCAR (*Puts in money*)   You got a big mouth, Murray. Just for that, lend me twenty dollars.

> (SPEED *deals another round*)

MURRAY I just loaned you twenty dollars ten minutes ago.

 (*They all join in a round of betting*)

OSCAR You loaned me *ten* dollars *twenty* minutes ago. Learn to count, pussycat.

MURRAY Learn to play poker, chicken licken! Borrow from somebody else. I keep winning my own money back.

ROY (*To* OSCAR) You owe everybody in the game. If you don't have it, you shouldn't play.

OSCAR All right, I'm through being the nice one. You owe me six dollars apiece for the buffet.

SPEED (*Dealing another round of cards*) Buffet? Hot beer and two sandwiches left over from when you went to high school?

OSCAR What do you want at a poker game, a tomato surprise? Murray, lend me twenty dollars or I'll call your wife and tell her you're in Central Park wearing a dress.

MURRAY You want money, ask Felix.

OSCAR He's not here.

MURRAY Neither am I.

ROY (*Gives him money*) All right, here. You're on the books for another twenty.

OSCAR How many times are you gonna keep saying it?
 (*He takes the money*)

MURRAY When are you gonna call Felix?

OSCAR When are we gonna play poker?

MURRAY Aren't you even worried? It's the first game he's missed in over two years.

OSCAR The record is fifteen years set by Lou Gehrig in
1939! I'll call! I'll call!

ROY How can you be so lazy?
(*The phone rings*)

OSCAR (*Throwing his cards in*) Call me irresponsible,
I'm funny that way.
(*He goes to the phone*)

SPEED Pair of sixes . . .

VINNIE Three deuces . . .

SPEED (*Throws up his hands in despair*) This is my last
week. I get all the aggravation I need at home.
(OSCAR *picks up the phone*)

OSCAR Hello! Oscar the Poker Player!

VINNIE (*To* OSCAR) If it's my wife tell her I'm leaving at
twelve.

SPEED (*To* VINNIE) You look at your watch once more
and you get the peanuts in your face. (*To* ROY) Deal the
cards!
(*The game continues during* OSCAR's *phone conversation, with* ROY *dealing a game of stud*)

OSCAR (*Into the phone*) Who? Who did you want,
please? *Dabby?* Dabby who? No, there's no Dabby
here. Oh, *Daddy!* (*To the others*) For crise sakes, it's my
kid. (*Back into the phone, he speaks with great love and
affection*) Brucey, hello, baby. Yes, it's Daddy! (*There
is a general outburst of ad libbing from the poker players. To the others*) Hey, come on, give me a break,
willya? My five-year-old kid is calling from California.
It must be costing him a fortune. (*Back into the phone*)
How've you been, sweetheart? Yes, I finally got your
letter. It took three weeks. Yes, but next time you tell

11

Mommy to give you a stamp. I know, but you're not supposed to draw it on. (*He laughs. To the others*) You hear?

SPEED   We hear. We hear. We're all thrilled.

OSCAR   (*Into the phone*) What's that, darling? What goldfish? Oh, in your room! Oh, sure. Sure I'm taking care of them. (*He holds the phone over his chest*) Oh, God, I killed my kid's goldfish! (*Back into the phone*) Yes, I feed them every day.

ROY   Murderer!

OSCAR   Mommy wants to speak to me? Right. Take care of yourself, soldier. I love you.

VINNIE   (*Beginning to deal a game of stud*) Ante a dollar . . .

SPEED   (*To* OSCAR) Cost you a dollar to play. You got a dollar?

OSCAR   Not after I get through talking to this lady. (*Into the phone with false cheerfulness*) Hello, Blanche. How are you? Err, yes, I have a pretty good idea why you're calling. I'm a week behind with the check, right? *Four* weeks? That's not possible. Because it's not possible. Blanche, I keep a record of every check and I *know* I'm only *three* weeks behind! Blanche, I'm trying the best I can. Blanche, don't threaten me with jail because it's not a threat. With my expenses and my alimony, a prisoner takes home more pay than I do! Very nice, in front of the kids. Blanche, don't tell me you're going to have my salary attached, just say goodbye! Goodbye! (*He hangs up. To the players*) I'm eight hundred dollars behind in alimony so let's up the stakes.

(*He gets his drink from the poker table*)

ROY   She can do it, you know.

OSCAR   What?

ROY   Throw you in jail. For nonsupport of the kids.

OSCAR   Never. If she can't call me once a week to aggravate me, she's not happy.
  (*He crosses to the bar*)

MURRAY   It doesn't bother you? That you can go to jail? Or that maybe your kids don't have enough clothes or enough to eat?

OSCAR   Murray, *Poland* could live for a year on what my kids leave over from lunch! Can we play cards?
  (*He refills his drink*)

ROY   But that's the point. You shouldn't *be* in this kind of trouble. It's because you don't know how to manage anything. I should know; I'm your accountant.

OSCAR   (*Crossing to the table*)   If you're my accountant, how come I need money?

ROY   If you need money, how come you play poker?

OSCAR   Because I need money.

ROY   But you always lose.

OSCAR   That's why I need the money! Listen, *I'm* not complaining. *You're* complaining. I get along all right. I'm living.

ROY   Alone? In eight dirty rooms?

OSCAR   If I win tonight, I'll buy a broom.
  (MURRAY *and* SPEED *buy chips from* VINNIE, *and* MURRAY *begins to shuffle the deck for a game of draw*)

ROY   That's not what you need. What you need is a wife.

13

OSCAR How can I afford a wife when I can't afford a broom?

ROY Then don't play poker.

OSCAR (*Puts down his drink, rushes to* ROY *and they struggle over the bag of potato chips, which rips, showering everyone. They all begin to yell at one another*) Then don't come to my house and eat my potato chips!

MURRAY What are you yelling about? We're playing a friendly game.

SPEED Who's *playing*? We've been sitting here talking since eight o'clock.

VINNIE Since *seven*. That's why I said I was going to quit at *twelve*.

SPEED How'd you like a stale banana right in the mouth?

MURRAY (*The peacemaker*) All right, all right, let's calm down. Take it easy. I'm a cop, you know. I could arrest the whole lousy game. (*He finishes dealing the cards*) Four . . .

OSCAR (*Sitting at the table*) My friend Murray the Cop is right. Let's just play cards. And please hold them up; I can't see where I marked them.

MURRAY You're worse than the kids from the PAL.

OSCAR But you still love me, Roy, sweety, right?

ROY (*Petulant*) Yeah, yeah.

OSCAR That's not good enough. Come on, say it. In front of the whole poker game. "I love you, Oscar Madison."

ROY You don't take any of this seriously, do you? You owe money to your wife, your government, your friends . . .

OSCAR (*Throws his cards down*)   What do you want me to do, Roy, jump in the garbage disposal and grind myself to death? (*The phone rings. He goes to answer it*) Life goes on even for those of us who are divorced, broke and sloppy. (*Into the phone*) Hello? Divorced, Broke and Sloppy. Oh, hello, sweetheart. (*He becomes very seductive, pulls the phone to the side and talks low, but he is still audible to the others, who turn and listen*) I told you not to call me during the game. I can't talk to you now. You *know* I do, darling. All right, just a minute. (*He turns*) Murray, it's your wife.

> (*He puts the phone on the table and sits on the sofa*)

MURRAY (*Nods disgustedly as he crosses to the phone*) I wish you *were* having an affair with her. Then she wouldn't bother *me* all the time. (*He picks up the phone*) Hello, Mimi, what's wrong?

> (SPEED *gets up, stretches and goes into the bathroom*)

OSCAR (*In a woman's voice, imitating* MIMI)   What time are you coming home? (*Then imitating* MURRAY) I don't know, about twelve, twelve-thirty.

MURRAY (*Into the phone*)   I don't know, about twelve, twelve-thirty! (ROY *gets up and stretches*) Why, what did you want, Mimi? "A corned beef sandwich and a strawberry malted!"

OSCAR   Is she pregnant again?

MURRAY (*Holds the phone over his chest*)   No, just fat! (*There is the sound of a toilet flushing, and after* SPEED *comes out of the bathroom,* VINNIE *goes in. Into the phone again*) What? How could you hear that, I had the phone over my chest? Who? Felix? No, he didn't show up tonight. What's wrong? You're kidding! How should I know? All right, all right, goodbye. (*The toilet flushes again, and after* VINNIE *comes out of the bathroom,* ROY *goes in*) Goodbye, Mimi. Goodbye. (*He hangs up. To the others*) Well, what did I tell you? I knew it!

ROY   What's the matter?

MURRAY (*Pacing by the couch*)   Felix is missing!

OSCAR   Who?

MURRAY   Felix! Felix Ungar! The man who sits in that chair every week and cleans ashtrays. I told you something was up.

SPEED (*At the table*)   What do you mean, missing?

MURRAY   He didn't show up for work today. He didn't come home tonight. No one knows where he is. Mimi just spoke to his wife.

VINNIE (*In his chair at the poker table*)   Felix?

MURRAY   They looked everywhere. I'm telling you he's missing.

OSCAR   Wait a minute. No one is missing for one day.

VINNIE   That's right. You've got to be missing for forty-eight hours before you're missing. The worst he could be is lost.

MURRAY   How could he be lost? He's forty-four years old and lives on West End Avenue. What's the matter with you?

ROY (*Sitting in an armchair*)   Maybe he had an accident.

OSCAR   They would have heard.

ROY   If he's laying in a gutter somewhere? Who would know who he is?

OSCAR   He's got ninety-two credit cards in his wallet. The minute something happens to him, America lights up.

VINNIE   Maybe he went to a movie. You know how long those pictures are today.

SPEED   (*Looks at* VINNIE *contemptuously*)   No wonder you're going to Florida in July! Dumb, dumb, dumb!

ROY   Maybe he was mugged?

OSCAR   For thirty-six hours? How much money could he have on him?

ROY   Maybe they took his clothes. I knew a guy who was mugged in a doctor's office. He had to go home in a nurse's uniform.
      (OSCAR *throws a pillow from the couch at* ROY)

SPEED   Murray, you're a cop. What do you think?

MURRAY   I think it's something real bad.

SPEED   How do you know?

MURRAY   I can feel it in my bones.

SPEED (*To the others*)   You hear? Bulldog Drummond.

ROY   Maybe he's drunk. Does he drink?

OSCAR   Felix? On New Year's Eve he has Pepto-Bismal. What are we guessing? I'll call his wife.
      (*He picks up the phone*)

SPEED   Wait a minute! Don't start anything yet. Just 'cause we don't know where he is doesn't mean somebody else doesn't. Does he have a girl?

VINNIE   A what?

SPEED   A girl? You know. Like when you're through work early.

17

MURRAY   Felix? Playing around? Are you crazy? He wears a vest and galoshes.

SPEED   (*Gets up and moves toward* MURRAY)   You mean you automatically know who has and who hasn't got a girl on the side?

MURRAY   (*Moves to* SPEED)   Yes, I automatically know.

SPEED   All right, you're so smart. Have I got a girl?

MURRAY   No, you haven't got a girl. What you've got is what *I've* got. What you *wish* you got and what you *got* is a whole different civilization! *Oscar* maybe has a girl on the side.

SPEED   That's different. He's divorced. That's not on the side. That's in the middle.
    (*He moves to the table*)

OSCAR   (*To them both as he starts to dial*)   You through? 'Cause one of our poker players is missing. I'd like to find out about him.

VINNIE   I thought he looked edgy the last couple of weeks. (*To* SPEED) Didn't you think he looked edgy?

SPEED   No. As a matter of fact, I thought *you* looked edgy.
    (*He moves down to the right*)

OSCAR   (*Into the phone*)   Hello? Frances? Oscar. I just heard.

ROY   Tell her not to worry. She's probably hysterical.

MURRAY   Yeah, you know women.
    (*He sits down on the couch*)

OSCAR   (*Into the phone*)   Listen, Frances, the most important thing is not to worry. Oh! (*To the others*) She's not worried.

MURRAY   Sure.

OSCAR (*Into the phone*) Frances, do you have *any* idea where he could be? He what? You're kidding? Why? No, I didn't know. Gee, that's too bad. All right, listen, Frances, you just sit tight and the minute I hear anything I'll let you know. Right. G'bye.
>   (*He hangs up. They all look at him expectantly. He gets up wordlessly and crosses to the table, thinking. They all watch him a second, not being able to stand it any longer*)

MURRAY Ya gonna tell us or do we hire a private detective?

OSCAR They broke up!

ROY Who?

OSCAR Felix and Frances! They broke up! The entire marriage is through.

VINNIE You're kidding!

ROY I don't believe it.

SPEED After twelve years?
>   (OSCAR *sits down at the table*)

VINNIE They were such a happy couple.

MURRAY Twelve years doesn't mean you're a *happy* couple. It just means you're a *long* couple.

SPEED Go figure it. Felix and Frances.

ROY What are you surprised at? He used to sit there every Friday night and tell us how they were fighting.

SPEED I know. But who believes Felix?

VINNIE What happened?

OSCAR She wants out, that's all.

MURRAY   He'll go to pieces. I know Felix. He's going to try something crazy.

SPEED   That's all he ever used to talk about. "My beautiful wife. My wonderful wife." What happened?

OSCAR   His beautiful, wonderful wife can't stand him, that's what happened.

MURRAY   He'll kill himself. You hear what I'm saying? He's going to go out and try to kill himself.

SPEED (*To* MURRAY)   Will you shut up, Murray? Stop being a cop for two minutes. (*To* OSCAR) Where'd he go, Oscar?

OSCAR   He went out to kill himself.

MURRAY   What did I tell you?

ROY (*To* OSCAR)   Are you serious?

OSCAR   That's what she said. He was going out to kill himself. He didn't want to do it at home 'cause the kids were sleeping.

VINNIE   Why?

OSCAR   Why? Because that's Felix, that's why. (*He goes to the bar and refills his drink*) You know what he's like. He sleeps on the window sill. "Love me or I'll jump." 'Cause he's a nut, that's why.

MURRAY   That's right. Remember he tried something like that in the army? She wanted to break off the engagement so he started cleaning guns in his mouth.

SPEED   I don't believe it. Talk! That's all Felix is, talk.

VINNIE (*Worried*)   But is that what he said? In those words? "I'm going to kill myself?"

OSCAR (*Pacing about the table*) I don't know in what words. She didn't read it to me.

ROY You mean he left her a note?

OSCAR No, he sent a telegram.

MURRAY A *suicide telegram?* Who sends a suicide telegram?

OSCAR Felix, the nut, that's who! Can you imagine getting a thing like that? She even has to tip the kid a quarter.

ROY I don't get it. If he wants to kill himself, why does he send a telegram?

OSCAR Don't you see how his mind works? If he sends a note, she might not get it till Monday and he'd have no excuse for not being dead. This way, for a dollar ten, he's got a chance to be saved.

VINNIE You mean he really doesn't want to kill himself? He just wants sympathy.

OSCAR What he'd really like is to go to the funeral and sit in the back. He'd be the biggest crier there.

MURRAY He's right.

OSCAR Sure I'm right.

MURRAY We get these cases every day. All they want is attention. We got a guy who calls us every Saturday afternoon from the George Washington Bridge.

ROY I don't know. You never can tell what a guy'll do when he's hysterical.

MURRAY Nahhh. Nine out of ten times they don't jump.

ROY What about the tenth time?

MURRAY They jump. He's right. There's a possibility.

OSCAR   Not with Felix. I know him. He's too nervous to kill himself. He wears his seatbelt in a drive-in movie.

VINNIE   Isn't there someplace we could look for him?

SPEED   Where? Where would you look? Who knows where he is?
(*The doorbell rings. They all look at* OSCAR)

OSCAR   Of course! If you're going to kill yourself, where's the safest place to do it? With your friends!
(VINNIE *starts for the door*)

MURRAY (*Stopping him*)   Wait a minute! The guy may be hysterical. Let's play it nice and easy. If *we're* calm, maybe *he'll* be calm.

ROY (*Getting up and joining them*)   That's right. That's how they do it with those guys out on the ledge. You talk nice and soft.
(SPEED *rushes over to them, and joins in the frenzied discussion*)

VINNIE   What'll we say to him?

MURRAY   We don't say nothin'. Like we never heard a thing.

OSCAR (*Trying to get their attention*)   You through with this discussion? Because he already could have hung himself out in the hall. (*To* VINNIE) Vinnie, open the door!

MURRAY   Remember! Like we don't know nothin'.
(*They all rush back to their seats and grab up cards, which they concentrate on with the greatest intensity.* VINNIE *opens the door.* FELIX UNGAR *is there. He's about forty-four. His clothes are rumpled as if he had slept in them, and he needs a shave. Al-*

*though he tries to act matter-of-fact, there is an air
of great tension and nervousness about him)*

FELIX *(Softly)* Hi, Vin! *(*VINNIE *quickly goes back to his
seat and studies his cards.* FELIX *has his hands in his
pockets, trying to be very nonchalant. With controlled
calm)* Hi, fellas. *(They all mumble hello, but do not
look at him. He puts his coat over the railing and crosses
to the table)* How's the game going? *(They all mumble
appropriate remarks, and continue staring at their cards)*
Good! Good! Sorry I'm late. *(*FELIX *looks a little disap-
pointed that no one asks "What?" He starts to pick up a
sandwich, changes his mind and makes a gesture of dis-
taste. He vaguely looks around)* Any Coke left?

OSCAR *(Looking up from his cards)* Coke? Gee, I don't
think so. I got a Seven-Up!

FELIX *(Bravely)* No, I felt like a Coke. I just don't feel
like Seven-Up tonight!
(He stands watching the game)

OSCAR What's the bet?

SPEED You bet a quarter. It's up to Murray. Murray, what
do you say? *(*MURRAY *is staring at* FELIX*)* Murray!
Murray!

ROY *(To* VINNIE*)* Tap his shoulder.

VINNIE *(Taps* MURRAY's *shoulder)* Murray!

MURRAY *(Startled)* What? What?

SPEED It's up to you.

MURRAY Why is it always up to me?

SPEED It's not always up to you. It's up to you now. What
do you do?

MURRAY I'm in. I'm in.
(*He throws in a quarter*)

FELIX (*Moves to the bookcase*) Anyone call about me?

OSCAR Er, not that I can remember. (*To the others*) Did anyone call for Felix? (*They all shrug and ad lib "No"*) Why? Were you expecting a call?

FELIX (*Looking at the books on the shelf*) No! No! Just asking.
(*He opens a book and examines it*)

ROY Er, I'll see his bet and raise it a dollar.

FELIX (*Without looking up from the book*) I just thought someone might have called.

SPEED It costs me a dollar and a quarter to play, right?

OSCAR Right!

FELIX (*Still looking at the book, in a sing-song*) But, if no one called, no one called.
(*He slams the book shut and puts it back. They all jump at the noise*)

SPEED (*Getting nervous*) What does it cost me to play again?

MURRAY (*Angry*) A dollar and a quarter! *A dollar and a quarter!* Pay attention, for crise sakes!

ROY All right, take it easy. Take it easy.

OSCAR Let's calm down, everyone, heh?

MURRAY I'm sorry. I can't help it. (*Points to* SPEED) He makes me nervous.

SPEED I make *you* nervous. You make *me* nervous. You make *everyone* nervous.

24

MURRAY (*Sarcastic*) I'm sorry. Forgive me. I'll kill myself.

OSCAR Murray!
(*He motions with his head to* FELIX)

MURRAY (*Realizes his error*) Oh! Sorry.
(SPEED *glares at him. They all sit in silence a moment, until* VINNIE *catches sight of* FELIX, *who is now staring out an upstage window. He quickly calls the others' attention to* FELIX)

FELIX (*Looking back at them from the window*) Gee, it's a pretty view from here. What is it, twelve floors?

OSCAR (*Quickly crossing to the window and closing it*) No. It's only eleven. That's all. Eleven. It says twelve but it's really only eleven. (*He then turns and closes the other window as* FELIX *watches him.* OSCAR *shivers slightly*) Chilly in here. (*To the others*) Isn't it chilly in here?
(*He crosses back to the table*)

ROY Yeah, that's much better.

OSCAR (*To* FELIX) Want to sit down and play? It's still early.

VINNIE Sure. We're in no rush. We'll be here till three, four in the morning.

FELIX (*Shrugs*) I don't know; I just don't feel much like playing now.

OSCAR (*Sitting at the table*) Oh! Well, what *do* you feel like doing?

FELIX (*Shrugs*) I'll find *something*. (*He starts to walk toward the other room*) Don't worry about me.

OSCAR Where are you going?

FELIX (*Stops in the doorway. He looks at the others who are all staring at him*) To the john.

OSCAR (*Looks at the others, worried, then at* FELIX) Alone?

FELIX (*Nods*) I always go alone! Why?

OSCAR (*Shrugs*) No reason. You gonna be in there long?

FELIX (*Shrugs, then says meaningfully, like a martyr*) As long as it takes.
> (*Then he goes into the bathroom and slams the door shut behind him. Immediately they all jump up and crowd about the bathroom door, whispering in frenzied anxiety*)

MURRAY Are you crazy? Letting him go to the john alone?

OSCAR What did you want me to do?

ROY Stop him! Go in with him!

OSCAR Suppose he just has to go to the john?

MURRAY Supposing he does? He's better off being embarrassed than dead!

OSCAR How's he going to kill himself in the john?

SPEED What do you mean, how? Razor blades, pills. Anything that's in there.

OSCAR That's the kids' bathroom. The worst he could do is brush his teeth to death.

ROY He could jump.

VINNIE That's right. Isn't there a window in there?

OSCAR It's only six inches wide.

MURRAY He could break the glass. He could cut his wrists.

OSCAR He could also flush himself into the East River. I'm telling you he's not going to try anything!
(*He moves to the table*)

ROY (*Goes to the doorway*) Shhh! Listen! He's crying. (*There is a pause as all listen as* FELIX *sobs*) You hear that. He's crying.

MURRAY Isn't that terrible? For God's sakes, Oscar, do something! Say something!

OSCAR What? What do you say to a man who's crying in your bathroom?
(*There is the sound of the toilet flushing and* ROY *makes a mad dash back to his chair*)

ROY He's coming!
(*They all scramble back to their places.* MURRAY *gets mixed up with* VINNIE *and they quickly straighten it out.* FELIX *comes back into the room. But he seems calm and collected, with no evident sign of having cried*)

FELIX I guess I'll be running along.
(*He starts for the door.* OSCAR *jumps up. So do the others*)

OSCAR Felix, wait a second.

FELIX No! No! I can't talk to you. I can't talk to anyone. (*They all try to grab him, stopping him near the stairs*)

MURRAY Felix, please. We're your friends. Don't run out like this.
(FELIX *struggles to pull away*)

OSCAR Felix, sit down. Just for a minute. Talk to us.

FELIX There's nothing to talk about. There's nothing to say. It's over. Over. Everything is over. Let me go!

27

(*He breaks away from them and dashes into the stage-right bedroom. They start to chase him and he dodges from the bedroom through the adjoining door into the bathroom*)

ROY Stop him! Grab him!

FELIX (*Looking for an exit*) Let me out! I've got to get out of here!

OSCAR Felix, you're hysterical.

FELIX Please let me out of here!

MURRAY The john! Don't let him get in the john!

FELIX (*Comes out of the bathroom with* ROY *hanging onto him, and the others trailing behind*) Leave me alone. Why doesn't everyone leave me alone?

OSCAR All right, Felix, I'm warning you. Now cut it out! (*He throws a half-filled glass of water, which he has picked up from the bookcase, into* FELIX's *face*)

FELIX It's *my* problem. I'll work it out. Leave me alone. Oh, my stomach.
(*He collapses in* ROY's *arms*)

MURRAY What's the matter with your stomach?

VINNIE He looks sick. Look at his face.
(*They all try to hold him as they lead him over to the couch*)

FELIX I'm not sick. I'm all right. I didn't take anything, I swear. Ohh, my stomach.

OSCAR What do you mean you didn't take anything? What did you take?

FELIX (*Sitting on the couch*) Nothing! Nothing! I didn't take anything. Don't tell Frances what I did, please! Oohh, my stomach.

MURRAY He took something! I'm telling you he took
something.

OSCAR What, Felix? *What?*

FELIX Nothing! I didn't take anything.

OSCAR Pills? Did you take pills?

FELIX No! No!

OSCAR (*Grabbing* FELIX) Don't lie to me, Felix. Did you
take pills?

FELIX No, I didn't. I didn't take anything.

MURRAY Thank God he didn't take pills.
(*They all relax and take a breath of relief*)

FELIX Just a few, that's all.
(*They all react in alarm and concern over the pills*)

OSCAR He took pills.

MURRAY How many pills?

OSCAR What kind of pills?

FELIX I don't know what kind. Little green ones. I just
grabbed anything out of her medicine cabinet. I must
have been crazy.

OSCAR Didn't you look? Didn't you see what kind?

FELIX I couldn't see. The light's broken. Don't call
Frances. Don't tell her. I'm so ashamed. So ashamed.

OSCAR Felix, how many pills did you take?

FELIX I don't know. I can't remember.

OSCAR I'm calling Frances.

FELIX (*Grabs him*) No! Don't call her. Don't call her. If
she hears I took a whole bottle of pills . . .

MURRAY   A whole bottle? *A whole bottle of pills?* (*He turns to* VINNIE) My God, call an ambulance!
   (VINNIE *runs to the front door*)

OSCAR (*To* MURRAY)   You don't even know what *kind!*

MURRAY   What's the difference? He took a whole bottle!

OSCAR   Maybe they were vitamins. He could be the healthiest one in the room! Take it easy, will you?

FELIX   Don't call Frances. Promise me you won't call Frances.

MURRAY   Open his collar. Open the window. Give him some air.

SPEED   Walk him around. Don't let him go to sleep.
   (SPEED *and* MURRAY *pick* FELIX *up and walk him around, while* ROY *rubs his wrists*)

ROY   Rub his wrists. Keep his circulation going.

VINNIE (*Running to the bathroom to get a compress*)   A cold compress. Put a cold compress on his neck.
   (*They sit* FELIX *in the armchair, still chattering in alarm*)

OSCAR   One doctor at a time, heh? All the interns shut the hell up!

FELIX   I'm all right. I'll be all right. (*To* OSCAR *urgently*) You didn't call Frances, did you?

MURRAY (*To the others*)   You just gonna stand here? No one's gonna do anything? I'm calling a doctor.
   (*He crosses to the phone*)

FELIX   No! No doctor.

MURRAY   You *gotta* have a doctor.

FELIX   I don't need a doctor.

MURRAY   You gotta get the pills out.

FELIX   I got them out. I threw up before! (*He sits back weakly.* MURRAY *hangs up the phone*) Don't you have a root beer or a ginger ale?
    (VINNIE *gives the compress to* SPEED)

ROY (*To* VINNIE)   Get him a drink.

OSCAR (*Glares angrily at* FELIX)   He threw them up!

VINNIE   Which would you rather have, Felix, the root beer or the ginger ale?

SPEED (*To* VINNIE)   Get him the drink! Just get him the drink.
    (VINNIE *runs into the kitchen as* SPEED *puts the compress on* FELIX's *head*)

FELIX   Twelve years. Twelve years we were married. Did you know we were married twelve years, Roy?

ROY (*Comforting him*)   Yes, Felix. I knew.

FELIX (*With great emotion in his voice*)   And now it's over. Like that, it's over. That's hysterical, isn't it?

SPEED   Maybe it was just a fight. You've had fights before, Felix.

FELIX   No, it's over. She's getting a lawyer tomorrow. *My* cousin. She's using *my* cousin! (*He sobs*) Who am I going to get?
    (VINNIE *comes out of the kitchen with a glass of root beer*)

MURRAY (*Patting his shoulder*)   It's okay, Felix. Come on. Take it easy.

VINNIE (*Gives the glass to* FELIX)   Here's the root beer.

FELIX   I'm all right, honestly. I'm just crying.

(*He puts his head down. They all look at him helplessly*)

MURRAY   All right, let's not stand around looking at him. (*Pushes* SPEED *and* VINNIE *away*) Let's break it up, heh?

FELIX   Yes, don't stand there looking at me. Please.

OSCAR (*To the others*)   Come on, he's all right. Let's call it a night.
   (MURRAY, SPEED *and* ROY *turn in their chips at the poker table, get their coats and get ready to go*)

FELIX   I'm so ashamed. Please, fellas, forgive me.

VINNIE (*Bending to* FELIX)   Oh, Felix, we—we understand.

FELIX   Don't say anything about this to anyone, Vinnie. Will you promise me?

VINNIE   I'm going to Florida tomorrow.

FELIX   Oh, that's nice. Have a good time.

VINNIE   Thanks.

FELIX (*Turns away and sighs in despair*)   We were going to go to Florida next winter. (*He laughs, but it's a sob*) Without the kids! Now they'll go without me.
   (VINNIE *gets his coat and* OSCAR *ushers them all to the door*)

MURRAY (*Stopping at the door*)   Maybe one of us should stay?

OSCAR   It's all right, Murray.

MURRAY   Suppose he tries something again?

OSCAR   He won't try anything again.

MURRAY   How do you *know* he won't try anything again?

FELIX (*Turns to* MURRAY) I won't try anything again. I'm very tired.

OSCAR (*To* MURRAY) You hear? He's very tired. He had a busy night. Good night, fellows.
(*They all ad lib goodbyes and leave. The door closes, but opens immediately and* ROY *comes back in*)

ROY If anything happens, Oscar, just call me.
(*He exits, and as the door starts to close, it reopens and* SPEED *comes in*)

SPEED I'm three blocks away. I could be here in five minutes.
(*He exits, and as the door starts to close, it reopens and* VINNIE *comes back in*)

VINNIE If you need me I'll be at the Meridian Motel in Miami Beach.

OSCAR You'll be the first one I'll call, Vinnie.
(VINNIE *exits. The door closes and then reopens as* MURRAY *comes back*)

MURRAY (*To* OSCAR) You're sure?

OSCAR I'm sure.

MURRAY (*Loudly to* FELIX, *as he gestures to* OSCAR *to come to the door*) Good night, Felix. Try to get a good night's sleep. I guarantee you things are going to look a lot brighter in the morning. (*To* OSCAR, *sotto voce*) Take away his belt and his shoe laces.
(*He nods and exits.* OSCAR *turns and looks at* FELIX *sitting in the armchair and slowly moves across the room. There is a moment's silence*)

OSCAR (*He looks at* FELIX *and sighs*) Ohh, Felix, Felix, Felix, Felix!

FELIX (*Sits with his head buried in his hands. He doesn't look up*) I know, I know, I know, I know! What am I going to do, Oscar?

OSCAR You're gonna wash down the pills with some hot, black coffee. (*He starts for the kitchen, then stops*) Do you think I could leave you alone for two minutes?

FELIX No, I don't think so! Stay with me, Oscar. Talk to me.

OSCAR A cup of black coffee. It'll be good for you. Come on in the kitchen. I'll sit on you.

FELIX Oscar, the terrible thing is, I think I still love her. It's a lousy marriage but I still love her. I didn't want this divorce.

OSCAR (*Sitting on the arm of the couch*) How about some Ovaltine? You like Ovaltine? With a couple of fig newtons or chocolate mallomars?

FELIX All right, so we didn't get along. But we had two wonderful kids, and a beautiful home. Didn't we, Oscar?

OSCAR How about vanilla wafers? Or Vienna fingers? I got everything.

FELIX What more does she want? What does *any* woman want?

OSCAR I want to know what *you* want. Ovaltine, coffee or tea. Then we'll get to the divorce.

FELIX It's not fair, damn it! It's just not fair! (*He bangs his fist on the arm of the chair angrily, then suddenly winces in great pain and grabs his neck*) Oh! Ohh, my neck. My neck!

OSCAR What? What?

FELIX (*He gets up and paces in pain. He is holding his*

twisted neck) It's a nerve spasm. I get it in the neck. Oh! Ohh, that hurts.

OSCAR (*Rushing to help*) Where? Where does it hurt?

FELIX (*Stretches out an arm like a halfback*) Don't touch me! Don't touch me!

OSCAR I just want to see where it hurts.

FELIX It'll go away. Just let me alone a few minutes. Ohh! Ohh!

OSCAR (*Moving to the couch*) Lie down; I'll rub it. It'll ease the pain.

FELIX (*In wild contortions*) You don't know how. It's a special way. Only Frances knows how to rub me.

OSCAR You want me to ask her to come over and rub you?

FELIX (*Yells*) No! No! We're getting divorced. She wouldn't want to rub me anymore. It's tension. I get it from tension. I must be tense.

OSCAR I wouldn't be surprised. How long does it last?

FELIX Sometimes a minute, sometimes hours. I once got it while I was driving. I crashed into a liquor store. Ohhh! Ohhh!
    (*He sits down, painfully, on the couch*)

OSCAR (*Getting behind him*) You want to suffer or do you want me to rub your stupid neck?
    (*He starts to massage it*)

FELIX Easy! Easy!

OSCAR (*Yells*) Relax, damn it: relax!

FELIX (*Yells back*) Don't yell at me! (*Then quietly*) What should I do? Tell me nicely.

OSCAR (*Rubbing the neck*) Think of warm jello!

35

FELIX Isn't that terrible? I can't do it. I can't relax. I sleep in one position all night. Frances says when I die on my tombstone it's going to say, "Here Stands Felix Ungar." (*He winces*) Oh! Ohh!

OSCAR (*Stops rubbing*) Does that hurt?

FELIX No, it feels good.

OSCAR Then say so. You make the same sound for pain or happiness.
    (*Starts to massage his neck again*)

FELIX I know. I know. Oscar—I think I'm crazy.

OSCAR Well, if it'll make you feel any better, I think so too.

FELIX I mean it. Why else do I go to pieces like this? Coming up here, scaring you to death. Trying to kill myself. What is that?

OSCAR That's panic. You're a panicky person. You have a low threshold for composure.
    (*He stops rubbing*)

FELIX Don't stop. It feels good.

OSCAR If you don't relax I'll break my fingers. (*Touches his hair*) Look at this. The only man in the world with clenched hair.

FELIX I do terrible things, Oscar. You know I'm a cry baby.

OSCAR Bend over.
    (FELIX *bends over and* OSCAR *begins to massage his back*)

FELIX (*Head down*) I tell the whole world my problems.

OSCAR (*Massaging hard*) Listen, if this hurts just tell me, because I don't know what the hell I'm doing.

FELIX It just isn't nice, Oscar, running up here like this, carrying on like a nut.

OSCAR (*Finishes massaging*) How does your neck feel?

FELIX (*Twists his neck*) Better. Only my back hurts. (*He gets up and paces, rubbing his back*)

OSCAR What you need is a drink. (*He starts for the bar*)

FELIX I can't drink. It makes me sick. I tried drinking last night.

OSCAR (*At the bar*) Where *were* you last night?

FELIX Nowhere. I just walked.

OSCAR All night?

FELIX All night.

OSCAR In the rain?

FELIX No. In a hotel. I couldn't sleep. I walked around the room all night. It was over near Times Square. A dirty, depressing room. Then I found myself looking out the window. And suddenly, I began to think about jumping.

OSCAR (*He has two glasses filled and crosses to* FELIX) What changed your mind?

FELIX Nothing. I'm still thinking about it.

OSCAR Drink this.
    (*He hands him a glass, crosses to the couch and sits*)

FELIX I don't want to get divorced, Oscar. I don't want to suddenly change my whole life. (*He moves to the couch*

37

and sits next to OSCAR) Talk to me, Oscar. What am I going to do? What am I going to do?

OSCAR You're going to pull yourself together. And then you're going to drink that Scotch, and then you and I are going to figure out a whole new life for you.

FELIX Without Frances? Without the kids?

OSCAR It's been done before.

FELIX (*Paces around*) You don't understand, Oscar. I'm nothing without them. I'm—*nothing!*

OSCAR What do you mean, nothing? You're something! (FELIX *sits in the armchair*) A person! You're flesh and blood and bones and hair and nails and ears. You're not a fish. You're not a buffalo. You're *you!* You walk and talk and cry and complain and eat little green pills and send suicide telegrams. No one else does that, Felix. I'm telling you, *you're the only one of its kind in the world!* (*He goes to the bar*) Now drink that.

FELIX Oscar, you've been through it yourself. What did you do? How did you get through those first few nights?

OSCAR (*Pours a drink*) I did exactly what you're doing.

FELIX Getting hysterical!

OSCAR No, drinking! *Drinking!* (*He comes back to the couch with the bottle and sits*) I drank for four days and four nights. And then I fell through a window. I was bleeding but I was forgetting.
(*He drinks again*)

FELIX How can you forget your kids? How can you wipe out twelve years of marriage?

OSCAR You can't. When you walk into eight empty rooms every night it hits you in the face like a wet glove. But those are the facts, Felix. You've got to face it. You can't spend the rest of your life crying. It annoys people in the movies! Be a good boy and drink your Scotch.

(*He stretches out on the couch with his head near* FELIX)

FELIX I can imagine what Frances must be going through.

OSCAR What do you mean, what *she's* going through?

FELIX It's much harder on the woman, Oscar. She's all alone with the kids. Stuck there in the house. She can't get out like me. I mean where is she going to find someone now at her age? With two kids. Where?

OSCAR I don't know. Maybe someone'll come to the door! Felix, there's a hundred thousand divorces a year. There must be *something* nice about it. (FELIX *suddenly puts both his hands over his ears and hums quietly*) What's the matter now?

(*He sits up*)

FELIX My ears are closing up. I get it from the sinus. It must be the dust in here. I'm allergic to dust.

(*He hums. Then he gets up and tries to clear his ears by hopping first on one leg then the other as he goes to the window and opens it*)

OSCAR (*Jumping up*) What are you doing?

FELIX I'm not going to jump. I'm just going to breathe. (*He takes deep breaths*) I used to drive Frances crazy with my allergies. I'm allergic to perfume. For a while the only thing she could wear was my after-shave lotion. I was impossible to live with. It's a wonder she took it this long.

(*He suddenly bellows like a moose. He makes this strange sound another time.* OSCAR *looks at him dumbfounded*)

39

OSCAR   What are you doing?

FELIX   I'm trying to clear my ears. You create a pressure inside and then it opens it up.
      (*He bellows again*)

OSCAR   Did it open up?

FELIX   A little bit. (*He rubs his neck*) I think I strained my throat.
      (*He paces about the room*)

OSCAR   Felix, why don't you leave yourself alone? Don't tinker.

FELIX   I can't help myself. I drive everyone crazy. A marriage counselor once kicked me out of his office. He wrote on my chart, "Lunatic!" I don't blame her. It's impossible to be married to me.

OSCAR   It takes two to make a rotten marriage.
      (*He lies back down on the couch*)

FELIX   You don't know what I was like at home. I bought her a book and made her write down every penny we spent. Thirty-eight cents for cigarettes; ten cents for a paper. Everything had to go in the book. And then we had a big fight because I said she forgot to write down how much the book was. Who could live with anyone like that?

OSCAR   An accountant! What do I know? We're not perfect. We all have faults.

FELIX   Faults? Heh! Faults. We have a maid who comes in to clean three times a week. And on the other days, Frances does the cleaning. And at night, after they've both cleaned up, I go in and clean the whole place again. I can't help it. I like things clean. Blame it on my mother. I was toilet-trained at five months old.

OSCAR How do you remember things like that?

FELIX I loused up the marriage. Nothing was ever right. I used to recook everything. The minute she walked out of the kitchen I would add salt or pepper. It's not that I didn't trust her, it's just that I was a better cook. Well, I cooked myself out of a marriage. (*He bangs his head with the palm of his hand three times*) *God damned idiot!*

     (*He sinks down in the armchair*)

OSCAR Don't do that; you'll get a headache.

FELIX I can't stand it, Oscar. I hate me. Oh, boy, do I hate me.

OSCAR You don't hate you. You love you. You think no one has problems like you.

FELIX Don't give me that analyst jazz. I happen to know I hate my guts.

OSCAR Come on, Felix; I've never *seen* anyone so in love.

FELIX (*Hurt*) I thought you were my friend.

OSCAR That's why I can talk to you like this. Because I love you almost as much as *you* do.

FELIX Then help me.

OSCAR (*Up on one elbow*) How can I help you when I can't help myself? You think *you're* impossible to live with? Blanche used to say, "What time do you want dinner?" And I'd say, "I don't know. I'm not hungry." Then at three o'clock in the morning I'd wake her up and say, "Now!" I've been one of the highest paid sportswriters in the East for the past fourteen years, and we saved eight and a half dollars—in pennies! I'm never home, I gamble, I burn cigar holes in the furniture, drink like a fish and lie to her every chance I get. And for our tenth wedding anniversary, I took her to see the New York Rangers-Detroit Red Wings hockey game where she got hit with a puck. And I *still* can't understand why she left me. That's how impossible *I* am!

FELIX   I'm not like you, Oscar. I couldn't take it living all alone. I don't know how I'm going to work. They've got to fire me. How am I going to make a living?

OSCAR   You'll go on street corners and cry. They'll throw nickels at you! You'll work, Felix; you'll work.
   (*He lies back down*)

FELIX   You think I ought to call Frances?

OSCAR   (*About to explode*)   What for?
   (*He sits up*)

FELIX   Well, talk it out again.

OSCAR   You've *talked* it all out. There are no words left in your entire marriage. When are you going to face up to it?

FELIX   I can't help it, Oscar; I don't know what to do.

OSCAR   Then listen to me. Tonight you're going to sleep here. And tomorrow you're going to get your clothes and your electric toothbrush and you'll move in with me.

FELIX   No, no. It's your apartment. I'll be in the way.

OSCAR   There's eight rooms. We could go for a year without seeing each other. Don't you understand? I *want* you to move in.

FELIX   Why? I'm a pest.

OSCAR   I *know* you're a pest. You don't have to keep telling me.

FELIX   Then why do you want me to live with you?

FELIX UNGAR, played by Art Carney, shows snapshots of his children to his dinner guests, CECILY and GWENDOLYN PIGEON, played by Monica Evans and Carole Shelley.

OSCAR Because I can't stand living alone, that's why! For crying out loud, I'm proposing to you. What do you want, a ring?

FELIX (*Moves to* OSCAR) Well, Oscar, if you really mean it, there's a lot I can do around here. I'm very handy around the house. I can fix things.

OSCAR You don't have to fix things.

FELIX I want to do *something*, Oscar. Let me do something.

OSCAR (*Nods*) All right, you can take my wife's initials off the towels. Anything you want.

FELIX (*Beginning to tidy up*) I can cook. I'm a terrific cook.

OSCAR You don't have to cook. I eat cold cuts for breakfast.

FELIX Two meals a day at home, we'll save a fortune. We've got to pay alimony, you know.

OSCAR (*Happy to see* FELIX's *new optimism*) All right, you can cook.
  (*He throws a pillow at him*)

FELIX (*Throws the pillow back*) Do you like leg of lamb?

OSCAR Yes, I like leg of lamb.

FELIX I'll make it tomorrow night. I'll have to call Frances. She has my big pot.

OSCAR *Will you forget Frances!* We'll get our own pots. Don't drive me crazy before you move in. (*The phone rings.* OSCAR *picks it up quickly*) Hello? Oh, hello, Frances!

FELIX (*Stops cleaning and starts to wave his arms wildly. He whispers screamingly*) I'm not here! I'm not here!

43

You didn't see me. You don't know where I am. I didn't call. I'm not here. I'm not here.

OSCAR (*Into the phone*)   Yes, he's here.

FELIX (*Pacing back and forth*)   How does she sound? Is she worried? Is she crying? What is she saying? Does she want to speak to me? I don't want to speak to her.

OSCAR (*Into the phone*)   Yes, he is!

FELIX   You can tell her I'm not coming back. I've made up my mind. I've had it there. I've taken just as much as she has. You can tell her for me if she thinks I'm coming back she's got another think coming. Tell her. Tell her.

OSCAR (*Into the phone*)   Yes! Yes, he's fine.

FELIX   Don't tell her I'm fine! You heard me carrying on before. What are you telling her that for? I'm not fine.

OSCAR (*Into the phone*)   Yes, I understand, Frances.

FELIX (*Sits down next to* OSCAR)   Does she want to speak to me? Ask her if she wants to speak to me?

OSCAR (*Into the phone*)   Do you want to speak to him?

FELIX (*Reaches for the phone*)   Give me the phone. I'll speak to her.

OSCAR (*Into the phone*)   Oh. You don't want to speak to him.

FELIX   She doesn't want to speak to me?

OSCAR (*Into the phone*)   Yeah, I see. Right. Well, goodbye.
(*He hangs up*)

FELIX   She didn't want to speak to me?

OSCAR   No!

FELIX   Why did she call?

OSCAR   She wants to know when you're coming over for your clothes. She wants to have the room repainted.

FELIX   Oh!

OSCAR   (*Pats* FELIX *on the shoulder*)   Listen, Felix, it's almost one o'clock.
   (*He gets up*)

FELIX   Didn't want to speak to me, huh?

OSCAR   I'm going to bed. Do you want a cup of tea with Fruitanos or Raisinettos?

FELIX   She'll paint it pink. She always wanted it pink.

OSCAR   I'll get you a pair of pajamas. You like stripes, dots, or animals?
   (*He goes into the bedroom*)

FELIX   She's really heartbroken, isn't she? I want to kill myself, and she's picking out colors.

OSCAR   (*In the bedroom*)   Which bedroom do you want? I'm lousy with bedrooms.

FELIX   (*Gets up and moves toward the bedroom*)   You know, I'm glad. Because she finally made me realize—it's over. It didn't sink in until just this minute.

OSCAR   (*Comes back with pillow, pillowcase, and pajamas*)   Felix, I want you to go to bed.

FELIX   I don't think I believed her until just now. My marriage is *really* over.

OSCAR   Felix, go to bed.

FELIX   Somehow it doesn't seem so bad now. I mean, I think I can live with this thing.

OSCAR   Live with it tomorrow. Go to bed tonight.

45

FELIX In a little while. I've got to think. I've got to start rearranging my life. Do you have a pencil and paper?

OSCAR Not in a little while. Now! It's my house; I make up the bedtime.
(*He throws the pajamas to him*)

FELIX Oscar, please. I have to be alone for a few minutes. I've got to get organized. Go on, you go to bed. I'll—I'll clean up.
(*He begins picking up debris from the floor*)

OSCAR (*Putting the pillow into the pillowcase*) You don't have to clean up. I pay a dollar fifty an hour to clean up.

FELIX It's all right, Oscar. I wouldn't be able to sleep with all this dirt around anyway. Go to bed. I'll see you in the morning.
(*He puts the dishes on the tray*)

OSCAR You're not going to do anything big, are you, like rolling up the rugs?

FELIX Ten minutes, that's all I'll be.

OSCAR You're sure?

FELIX (*Smiles*) I'm sure.

OSCAR No monkey business?

FELIX No monkey business. I'll do the dishes and go right to bed.

OSCAR Yeah.
(*Crosses up to his bedroom, throwing the pillow into the downstage bedroom as he passes. He closes his bedroom door behind him*)

FELIX (*Calls him*) Oscar! (OSCAR *anxiously comes out of his bedroom and crosses to* FELIX) I'm going to be all right! It's going to take me a couple of days, but I'm going to be all right.

OSCAR (*Smiles*) Good! Well, good night, Felix.
(*He turns to go toward the bedroom as* FELIX *begins to plump up a pillow from the couch*)

FELIX Good night, Frances.
(OSCAR *stops dead.* FELIX, *unaware of his error, plumps another pillow as* OSCAR *turns and stares at* FELIX *with a troubled expression*)

Curtain

Act Two

Two weeks later, about eleven at night. The poker game is in session again. VINNIE, ROY, SPEED, MURRAY *and* OSCAR *are all seated at the table.* FELIX's *chair is empty.*

There is one major difference between this scene and the opening poker-game scene. It is the appearance of the room. It is immaculately clean. No, not clean. Sterile! Spotless! Not a speck of dirt can be seen under the ten coats of Johnson's Glo-Coat that have been applied to the floor in the last three weeks. No laundry bags, no dirty dishes, no half-filled glasses.

Suddenly FELIX *appears from the kitchen. He carries a tray with glasses and food—and napkins. After putting the tray down, he takes the napkins one at a time, flicks them out to full length and hands one to every player. They take them with grumbling and put them on their laps. He picks up a can of beer and very carefully pours it into a tall glass, measuring it perfectly so that not a drop spills or overflows. With a flourish he puts the can down.*

FELIX (*Moves to* MURRAY) An ice-cold glass of beer for Murray.

     (MURRAY *reaches up for it*)

MURRAY Thank you, Felix.

FELIX (*Holds the glass back*) Where's your coaster?

MURRAY   My what?

FELIX   Your coaster. The little round thing that goes under the glass.

MURRAY (*Looks around on the table*)   I think I bet it.

OSCAR (*Picks it up and hands it to* MURRAY)   I knew I was winning too much. Here!

FELIX   Always try to use your coasters, fellows. (*He picks up another drink from the tray*) Scotch and a little bit of water?

SPEED (*Raises his hand*)   Scotch and a little bit of water. (*Proudly*) And I have my coaster.
　　　　(*He holds it up for inspection*)

FELIX (*Hands him the drink*)   I hate to be a pest but you know what wet glasses do?
　　　　(*He goes back to the tray and picks up and wipes a clean ashtray*)

OSCAR (*Coldly and deliberately*)   They leave little rings on the table.

FELIX (*Nods*)   Ruins the finish. Eats right through the polish.

OSCAR (*To the others*)   So let's watch those little rings, huh?

FELIX (*Takes an ashtray and a plate with a sandwich from the tray and crosses to the table*)   And we have a clean ashtray for Roy (*Handing* ROY *the ashtray*) Aaaaand—a sandwich for Vinnie.
　　　　(*Like a doting headwaiter, he skillfully places the sandwich in front of* VINNIE)

VINNIE (*Looks at* FELIX, *then at the sandwich*)   Gee, it smells good. What is it?

FELIX   Bacon, lettuce and tomato with mayonnaise on pumpernickel toast.

VINNIE (*Unbelievingly*)   Where'd you get it?

FELIX (*Puzzled*)   I made it. In the kitchen.

VINNIE   You mean you put in toast and cooked bacon? Just for me?

OSCAR   If you don't like it, he'll make you a meat loaf. Takes him five minutes.

FELIX   It's no trouble. Honest. I love to cook. Try to eat over the dish. I just vacuumed the rug. (*He goes back to the tray, then stops*) Oscar!

OSCAR (*Quickly*)   Yes, sir?

FELIX   I forgot what you wanted. What did you ask me for?

OSCAR   Two three-and-a-half-minute eggs and some petit fours.

FELIX (*Points to him*)   A double gin and tonic. I'll be right back. (FELIX *starts out, then stops at a little box on the bar*) Who turned off the Pure-A-Tron?

MURRAY   The what?

FELIX   The Pure-A-Tron! (*He snaps it back on*) Don't play with this, fellows. I'm trying to get some of the grime out of the air.
   (*He looks at them and shakes his head disapprovingly, then exits. They all sit in silence a few seconds*)

OSCAR   Murray, I'll give you two hundred dollars for your gun.

SPEED (*Throws his cards on the table and gets up angrily*)   I can't take it any more. (*With his hand on his neck*)

I've had it up to here. In the last three hours we played four minutes of poker. I'm not giving up my Friday nights to watch cooking and housekeeping.

ROY (*Slumped in his chair, head hanging down*) I can't breathe. (*He points to the Pure-A-Tron*) That lousy machine is sucking everything out of the air.

VINNIE (*Chewing*) Gee, this is delicious. Who wants a bite?

MURRAY Is the toast warm?

VINNIE Perfect. And not too much mayonnaise. It's really a well-made sandwich.

MURRAY Cut me off a little piece.

VINNIE Give me your napkin. I don't want to drop any crumbs.

SPEED (*Watches them, horrified, as* VINNIE *carefully breaks the sandwich over* MURRAY's *napkin. Then he turns to* OSCAR) Are you listening to this? Martha and Gertrude at the Automat. (*Almost crying in despair*) What the hell happened to our poker game?

ROY (*Still choking*) I'm telling you that thing could kill us. They'll find us here in the morning with our tongues on the floor.

SPEED (*Yells at* OSCAR) Do something! Get him back in the game.

OSCAR (*Rises, containing his anger*) Don't bother me with your petty little problems. You get this one stinkin' night a week. I'm cooped up here with Dione Lucas twenty-four hours a day.

(*He moves to the window*)

ROY It was better before. With the garbage and the smoke, it was better before.

VINNIE (*To* MURRAY) Did you notice what he does with the bread?

MURRAY What?

VINNIE He cuts off the crusts. That's why the sandwich is so light.

MURRAY And then he only uses the soft, green part of the lettuce. (*Chewing*) It's really delicious.

SPEED (*Reacts in amazement and disgust*) I'm going out of my mind.

OSCAR (*Yells toward the kitchen*) Felix! Damn it, *Felix!*

SPEED (*Takes the kitty box from the bookcase, puts it on the table, and puts the money in*) Forget it. I'm going home.

OSCAR Sit down!

SPEED I'll buy a book and I'll start to read again.

OSCAR Siddown! Will you siddown! (*Yells*) Felix!

SPEED Oscar, it's all over. The day his marriage busted up was the end of our poker game. (*He takes his jacket from the back of the chair and crosses to the door*) If you find some real players next week, call me.

OSCAR (*Following him*) You can't run out now. I'm a big loser.

SPEED (*With the door open*) You got no one to blame but yourself. It's all your fault. You're the one who stopped him from killing himself.

(*He exits and slams the door*)

OSCAR (*Stares at the door*) He's right! The man is absolutely right.

(*He moves to the table*)

MURRAY (*To* VINNIE) Are you going to eat that pickle?

VINNIE I wasn't thinking of it. Why? Do you want it?

MURRAY Unless you want it. It's your pickle.

VINNIE No, no. Take it. I don't usually eat pickle.

(VINNIE *holds the plate with the pickle out to* MURRAY. OSCAR *slaps the plate, which sends the pickle flying through the air*)

OSCAR Deal the cards!

MURRAY What did you do that for?

OSCAR Just deal the cards. You want to play poker, deal the cards. You want to eat, go to Schrafft's. (*To* VINNIE) Keep your sandwich and your pickles to yourself. I'm losing ninety-two dollars and everybody's getting fat! (*He screams*) Felix!

(FELIX *appears in the kitchen doorway*)

FELIX What?

OSCAR Close the kitchen and sit down. It's a quarter to twelve. I still got an hour and a half to win this month's alimony.

ROY (*Sniffs*) What is that smell? Disinfectant! (*He smells the cards*) It's the cards. *He washed the cards!* (*He throws down the cards, takes his jacket from the chair and moves past the table to put his money into the kitty box*)

FELIX (*Comes to the table with* OSCAR's *drink, which he puts down; then he sits in his own seat*) Okay. What's the bet?

OSCAR (*Hurrying to his seat*) I can't believe it. We're gonna play cards again. (*He sits*) It's up to Roy. Roy, baby, what are you gonna do?

ROY I'm going to get in a cab and go to Central Park. If I don't get some fresh air, you got yourself a dead accountant.

(*He moves toward the door*)

OSCAR (*Follows him*) What do you mean? It's not even twelve o'clock.

ROY (*Turns back to* OSCAR) Look, I've been sitting here breathing Lysol and ammonia for four hours! Nature didn't intend for poker to be played like that. (*He crosses to the door*) If you wanna have a game next week (*He points to* FELIX) either Louis Pasteur cleans up *after* we've gone, or we play in the Hotel Dixie! Good night!

(*He goes and slams the door. There is a moment's silence.* OSCAR *goes back to the table and sits*)

OSCAR We got just enough for handball!

FELIX Gee, I'm sorry. Is it my fault?

VINNIE No, I guess no one feels like playing much lately.

MURRAY Yeah. I don't know what it is, but something's happening to the old gang.

(*He goes to a side chair, sits and puts on his shoes*)

OSCAR Don't you know what's happening to the old gang? It's breaking up. Everyone's getting divorced. I swear, we used to have better games when we couldn't get out at night.

VINNIE (*Getting up and putting on his jacket*) Well, I guess I'll be going too. Bebe and I are driving to Asbury Park for the weekend.

57

FELIX   Just the two of you, heh? Gee, that's nice! You always do things like that together, don't you?

VINNIE (*Shrugs*)   We have to. I don't know how to drive! (*He takes all the money from the kitty box and moves to the door*) You coming, Murray?

MURRAY (*Gets up, takes his jacket and moves toward the door*)   Yeah, why not? If I'm not home by one o'clock with a hero sandwich and a frozen éclair, she'll have an all-points out on me. Ahhh, you guys got the life.

FELIX   Who?

MURRAY (*Turns back*)   Who? You! The Marx Brothers! Laugh, laugh, laugh. What have you got to worry about? If you suddenly want to go to the Playboy Club to hunt Bunnies, who's gonna stop you?

FELIX   I don't belong to the Playboy Club.

MURRAY   I know you don't, Felix, it's just a figure of speech. Anyway, it's not such a bad idea. Why don't you join?

FELIX   Why?

MURRAY   Why! Because for twenty-five dollars they give you a key—and you walk into Paradise. *My* keys cost thirty cents—and you walk into corned beef and cabbage. (*He winks at him*) Listen to me.
      (*He moves to the door*)

FELIX   What are you talking about, Murray? You're a happily married man.

MURRAY (*Turns back on the landing*)   I'm not talking about *my* situation. (*He puts on his jacket*) I'm talking about *yours!* Fate has just played a cruel and rotten trick on you, so enjoy it! (*He turns to go, revealing "PAL"*

letters sewn on the back of his jacket) C'mon, Vinnie.
(VINNIE *waves goodbye and they both exit)*

FELIX *(Staring at the door)* That's funny, isn't it, Oscar?
They think we're happy. They really think we're enjoy-
ing this. *(He gets up and begins to straighten up the
chairs)* They don't know, Oscar. They don't know what
it's like.
> *(He gives a short, ironic laugh, tucks the napkins
> under his arm and starts to pick up the dishes from
> the table)*

OSCAR I'd be immensely grateful to you, Felix, if you
didn't clean up just now.

FELIX *(Puts dishes on the tray)* It's only a few things.
(He stops and looks back at the door) I can't get over
what Murray just said. You know I think they really
envy us. *(He clears more stuff from the table)*

OSCAR Felix, leave everything alone. I'm not through
dirtying-up for the night.
> *(He drops some poker chips on the floor)*

FELIX *(Putting stuff on the tray)* But don't you see the
irony of it? Don't you see it, Oscar?

OSCAR *(Sighs heavily)* Yes, I see it.

FELIX *(Clearing the table)* No, you don't. I really don't
think you do.

OSCAR Felix, I'm telling you I see the irony of it.

FELIX *(Pauses)* Then tell me. What is it? What's the
irony?

OSCAR *(Deep breath)* The irony is—unless we can come
to some other arrangement, I'm gonna kill you! That's
the irony.

59

FELIX What's wrong?
(*He crosses back to the tray and puts down all the glasses and other things*)

OSCAR There's something wrong with this system, that's what's wrong. I don't think that two single men living alone in a big eight-room apartment should have a cleaner house than my mother.

FELIX (*Gets the rest of the dishes, glasses and coasters from the table*) What are you talking about? I'm just going to put the dishes in the sink. You want me to leave them here all night?

OSCAR (*Takes his glass, which* FELIX *has put on the tray, and crosses to the bar for a refill*) I don't care if you take them to bed with you. You can play Mr. Clean all you want. But don't make *me* feel guilty.

FELIX (*Takes the tray into the kitchen, leaving the swinging door open*) I'm not asking you to do it, Oscar. You don't have to clean up.

OSCAR (*Moves up to the door*) That's why you make me feel guilty. You're always in my bathroom hanging up my towels. Whenever I smoke you follow me around with an ashtray. Last night I found you washing the kitchen floor, shaking your head and moaning, "Footprints, footprints!"
(*He paces around the room*)

FELIX (*Comes back to the table with a silent butler. He dumps the ashtrays, then wipes them carefully*) I didn't say they were yours.

OSCAR (*Angrily sits down in the wing chair*) Well, they *were* mine, damn it. I have feet and they make prints. What do you want me to do, climb across the cabinets?

FELIX   No! I want you to walk on the floor.

OSCAR   I appreciate that! I really do.

FELIX   (*Crosses to the telephone table and cleans the ash-tray there*)   I'm just trying to keep the place livable. I didn't realize I irritated you that much.

OSCAR   I just feel *I* should have the right to decide when my bathtub needs a going over with Dutch Cleanser. It's the democratic way!

FELIX   (*Puts the silent butler and his rag down on the coffee table and sits down glumly on the couch*)   I was wondering how long it would take.

OSCAR   How long *what* would take?

FELIX   Before I got on your nerves.

OSCAR   I didn't say you get on my nerves.

FELIX   Well, it's the same thing. You said I irritated you.

OSCAR   *You* said you irritated me. *I* didn't say it.

FELIX   Then what *did* you say?

OSCAR   I don't know *what* I said. What's the difference what I said?

FELIX   It doesn't make any difference. I was just repeating what I thought you said.

OSCAR   Well, don't repeat what you *thought* I said. Repeat what I *said!* My God, that's irritating!

FELIX   You see! You *did* say it!

OSCAR   I don't believe this whole conversation.
(*He gets up and paces by the table*)

FELIX   (*Pawing with a cup*)   Oscar, I'm—I'm sorry. I don't know what's wrong with me.

OSCAR (*Still pacing*)   And don't pout. If you want to fight, we'll fight. But don't pout! Fighting *I* win. Pouting *you* win!

FELIX   You're right. Everything you say about me is absolutely right.

OSCAR (*Really angry, turns to* FELIX)   And don't give in so easily. I'm *not* always right. Sometimes *you're* right.

FELIX   You're right. I do that. I always figure I'm in the wrong.

OSCAR   Only this time you *are* wrong. And I'm right.

FELIX   Oh, leave me alone.

OSCAR   And don't sulk. That's the same as pouting.

FELIX   I know. I know. (*He squeezes his cup with anger*) Damn me, why can't I do one lousy thing right?
   (*He suddenly stands up and cocks his arm back, about to hurl the cup angrily against the front door. Then he thinks better of it, puts the cup down and sits*)

OSCAR (*Watching this*)   Why didn't you throw it?

FELIX   I almost did. I get so insane with myself sometimes.

OSCAR   Then why don't you throw the cup?

FELIX   Because I'm trying to control myself.

OSCAR   Why?

FELIX   What do you mean, why?

OSCAR   Why do you have to control yourself? You're angry, you felt like throwing the cup, why don't you throw it?

FELIX   Because there's no point to it. I'd still be angry and I'd have a broken cup.

OSCAR How do you *know* how you'd feel? Maybe you'd feel *wonderful*. Why do you have to control every single thought in your head? Why don't you let loose *once* in your life? Do something that you *feel* like doing—and not what you *think* you're supposed to do. Stop keeping books, Felix. Relax. Get drunk. Get angry. C'mon, *break the goddamned cup!*
 (FELIX *suddenly stands up and hurls the cup against the door, smashing it to pieces. Then he grabs his shoulder in pain*)

FELIX Oww! I hurt my arm!
 (*He sinks down on the couch, massaging his arm*)

OSCAR (*Throws up his hands*) You're hopeless! You're a hopeless mental case!
 (*He paces around the table*)

FELIX (*Grimacing with pain*) I'm not supposed to throw with that arm. What a stupid thing to do.

OSCAR Why don't you live in a closet? I'll leave your meals outside the door and slide in the papers. Is that safe enough?

FELIX (*Rubbing his arm*) I used to have bursitis in this arm. I had to give up golf. Do you have a heating pad?

OSCAR How can you hurt your arm throwing a cup? If it had coffee in it, that's one thing. But an empty cup . . .
 (*He sits in the wing chair*)

FELIX All right, cut it out, Oscar. That's the way I am. I get hurt easily. I can't help it.

OSCAR You're not going to cry, are you? I think all those tears dripping on the arm is what gave you bursitis.

FELIX (*Holding his arm*) I once got it just from combing my hair.

63

OSCAR (*Shaking his head*) A world full of room-mates and I pick myself the Tin Man. (*He sighs*) Oh, well, I suppose I could have done worse.

FELIX (*Moves the rag and silent butler to the bar. Then he takes the chip box from the bar and crosses to the table*) You're darn right, you could have. A *lot* worse.

OSCAR How?

FELIX What do you mean, how? How'd you like to live with ten-thumbs Murray or Speed and his complaining? (*He gets down on his knees, picks up the chips and puts them into the box*) Don't forget I cook and clean and take care of this house. I save us a lot of money, don't I?

OSCAR Yeah, but then you keep me up all night counting it.

FELIX (*Goes to the table and sweeps the chips and cards into the box*) Now wait a minute. We're not always going at each other. We have some fun too, don't we?

OSCAR (*Crosses to the couch*) Fun? Felix, getting a clear picture on Channel Two isn't my idea of whoopee.

FELIX What are you talking about?

OSCAR All right, what do you and I do every night?
(*He takes off his sneakers and drops them on the floor*)

FELIX What do we do? You mean after dinner?

OSCAR That's right. After we've had your halibut steak and the dishes are done and the sink has been Brillo'd and the pans have been S.O.S.'d and the leftovers have been Saran-Wrapped—what do we do?

FELIX (*Finishes clearing the table and puts everything on top of the bookcase*) Well, we read, we talk . . .

OSCAR (*Takes off his pants and throws them on the floor*) No, no. *I* read and *you* talk! I try to work and you talk. I take a bath and you talk. I go to sleep and you talk. We've got your life arranged pretty good but I'm still looking for a little entertainment.

FELIX (*Pulling the kitchen chairs away from the table*) What are you saying? That I talk too much?

OSCAR (*Sits on the couch*) No, no. I'm not complaining. You have a lot to say. What's worrying me is that I'm beginning to listen.

FELIX (*Pulls the table into the alcove*) Oscar, I told you a hundred times, just tell me to shut up. I'm not sensitive.
> (*He pulls the love seat down into the room, and centers the table between the windows in the alcove*)

OSCAR I don't think you're getting my point. For a husky man, I think I've spent enough evenings discussing tomorrow's menu. The night was made for other things.

FELIX Like what?
> (*He puts two dining chairs neatly on one side of the table*)

OSCAR Like unless I get to touch something soft in the next two weeks, I'm in big trouble.

FELIX You mean women?
> (*He puts the two other dining chairs neatly on the other side of the table*)

OSCAR If you want to give it a name, all right, women!

FELIX (*Picks up the two kitchen chairs and starts toward the landing*) That's funny. You know I haven't even *thought* about women in weeks.

65

OSCAR I fail to see the humor.

FELIX (*Stops*) No, that's really strange. I mean when Frances and I were happy, I don't think there was a girl on the street I didn't stare at for ten minutes. (*He crosses to the kitchen door and pushes it open with his back*) I used to take the wrong subway home just following a pair of legs. But since we broke up, I don't even know what a woman looks like.
(*He takes the chairs into the kitchen*)

OSCAR Well, either I could go downstairs and buy a couple of magazines—or I could make a phone call.

FELIX (*From the kitchen, as he washes the dishes*) What are you saying?

OSCAR (*Crosses to a humidor on a small table and takes out a cigar*) I'm saying let's spend one night talking to someone with higher voices than us.

FELIX You mean go out on a date?

OSCAR Yah . . .

FELIX Oh, well, I—I can't.

OSCAR Why not?

FELIX Well, it's all right for you. But I'm still married.

OSCAR (*Paces toward the kitchen door*) You can *cheat* until the divorce comes through!

FELIX It's not that. It's just that I have no—no *feeling* for it. I can't explain it.

OSCAR Try!

FELIX (*Comes to the doorway with a brush and dish in his hand*) Listen, I intend to go out. I get lonely too. But I'm just separated a few weeks. Give me a little time.
(*He goes back to the sink*)

OSCAR MADISON, played by Walter Matthau, confronts his roommate, FELIX UNGAR, played by Art Carney, nose to nose across the dining-room table.

OSCAR There isn't any time left. I saw *TV Guide* and there's nothing on this week! (*He paces into and through the kitchen and out the kitchen door onto the landing*) What am I asking you? All I want to do is have dinner with a couple of girls. You just have to eat and talk. It's not hard. You've eaten and talked before.

FELIX Why do you need me? Can't you go out yourself?

OSCAR Because I may want to come back here. And if we walk in and find you washing the windows, it puts a damper on things.
    (*He sits down*)

FELIX (*Pokes his head out of the kitchen*) I'll take a pill and go to sleep.
    (*He goes back into the kitchen*)

OSCAR Why take a pill when you can take a girl?

FELIX (*Comes out with an aerosol bomb held high over his head and circles around the room, spraying it*) Because I'd feel guilty, that's why. Maybe it doesn't make any sense to you, but that's the way I feel.
    (*He puts the bomb on the bar and takes the silent butler and rag into the kitchen. He places them on the sink and busily begins to wipe the refrigerator*)

OSCAR Look, for all I care you can take her in the kitchen and make a blueberry pie. But I think it's a lot healthier than sitting up in your bed every night writing Frances' name all through the crossword puzzles. Just for one night, talk to another girl.

FELIX (*Pushes the love seat carefully into position and sits, weakening*) But who would I call? The only single girl I know is my secretary and I don't think she likes me.

OSCAR (*Jumps up and crouches next to* FELIX) Leave that

67

to me. There's two sisters who live in this building. English girls. One's a widow; the other's a divorcée. They're a barrel of laughs.

FELIX How do you know?

OSCAR I was trapped in the elevator with them last week. (*Runs to the telephone table, puts the directory on the floor, and gets down on his knees to look for the number*) I've been meaning to call them but I didn't know which one to take out. This'll be perfect.

FELIX What do they look like?

OSCAR Don't worry. Yours is very pretty.

FELIX I'm not worried. Which one is mine?

OSCAR (*Looking in the book*) The divorcée.

FELIX (*Goes to* OSCAR) Why do I get the divorcée?

OSCAR I don't care. You want the widow?
(*He circles a number on the page with a crayon*)

FELIX (*Sitting on the couch*) No, I don't want the widow. I don't even want the divorcée. I'm just doing this for you.

OSCAR Look, take whoever you want. When they come in the door, point to the sister of your choice. (*Tears the page out of the book, runs to the bookcase and hangs it up*) I don't care. I just want to have some laughs.

FELIX All right. All right.

OSCAR (*Crosses to the couch and sits next to* FELIX) Don't say all right. I want you to promise me you're going to try to have a good time. Please, Felix. It's important. Say, "I promise."

FELIX (*Nods*) I promise.

OSCAR   Again!

FELIX   I promise!

OSCAR   And no writing in the book, a dollar thirty for the cab.

FELIX   No writing in the book.

OSCAR   No one is to be called Frances. It's Gwendolyn and Cecily.

FELIX   No Frances.

OSCAR   No crying, sighing, moaning or groaning.

FELIX   I'll smile from seven to twelve.

OSCAR   And this above all, no talk of the past. Only the present.

FELIX   And the future.

OSCAR   That's the new Felix I've been waiting for. (*Leaps up and prances around*) Oh, is this going to be a night. Hey, where do you want to go?

FELIX   For what?

OSCAR   For dinner. Where'll we eat?

FELIX   You mean a restaurant? For the four of us? It'll cost a fortune.

OSCAR   We'll cut down on laundry. We won't wear socks on Thursdays.

FELIX   But that's throwing away money. We can't afford it, Oscar.

OSCAR   We have to eat.

FELIX   (*Moves to* OSCAR)   We'll have dinner here.

OSCAR   *Here?*

FELIX   I'll cook. We'll save thirty, forty dollars.

(*He goes to the couch, sits and picks up the phone*)

OSCAR   What kind of a double date is that? You'll be in the kitchen all night.

FELIX   No, I won't. I'll put it up in the afternoon. Once I get my potatoes in, I'll have all the time in the world.
(*He starts to dial*)

OSCAR (*Pacing back and forth*)   What happened to the new Felix? Who are you calling?

FELIX   Frances. I want to get her recipe for London broil. The girls'll be crazy about it.
(*He dials as* OSCAR *storms off toward his bedroom*)

Curtain

SCENE 2

It is a few days later, about eight o'clock.

No one is on stage. The dining table looks like a page out of House and Garden. *It is set for dinner for four, complete with linen tablecloth, candles and wine glasses. There is a floral centerpiece and flowers about the room, and crackers and dip on the coffee table. There are sounds of activity in the kitchen.*

The front door opens and OSCAR *enters with a bottle of wine in a brown paper bag, his jacket over his arm. He looks about gleefully as he listens to the sounds from the kitchen. He puts the bag on the table and his jacket over a chair.*

OSCAR (*Calls out in a playful mood*) I'm home, dear! (*He goes into his bedroom, taking off his shirt, and comes skipping out shaving with a cordless razor, with a clean shirt and a tie over his arm. He is joyfully singing as he admires the table*) Beautiful! Just beautiful! (*He sniffs, obviously catching the aroma from the kitchen*) Oh, yeah. Something wonderful is going on in that kitchen. (*He rubs his hands gleefully*) No, sir. There's no doubt about it. I'm the luckiest man on earth. (*He puts the razor into his pocket and begins to put on the shirt.* FELIX *enters slowly from the kitchen. He's wearing a*

71

small dish towel as an apron. He has a ladle in one hand. He looks silently and glumly at OSCAR, *crosses to the armchair and sits*) I got the wine. (*He takes the bottle out of the bag and puts it on the table*) Batard Montrachet. Six and a quarter. You don't mind, do you, pussycat? We'll walk to work this week. (FELIX *sits glumly and silently*) Hey, no kidding, Felix, you did a great job. One little suggestion? Let's come down a little with the lights (*He switches off the wall brackets*) —and up very softly with the music. (*He crosses to the stereo set in the bookcase and picks up some record albums*) What do you think goes better with London broil, Mancini or Sinatra? (FELIX *just stares ahead*) Felix? What's the matter? (*He puts the albums down*) Something's wrong. I can tell by your conversation. (*He goes into the bathroom, gets a bottle of after-shave lotion and comes out putting it on*) All right, Felix, what is it?

FELIX (*Without looking at him*) What is it? Let's start with what time do you think it is?

OSCAR What time? I don't know. Seven thirty?

FELIX Seven thirty? Try eight o'clock.

OSCAR (*Puts the lotion down on the small table*) All right, so it's eight o'clock. So?
(*He begins to fix his tie*)

FELIX So? You said you'd be home at seven.

OSCAR Is that what I said?

FELIX (*Nods*) That's what you said. "I will be home at seven" is what you said.

OSCAR Okay, I said I'd be home at seven. And it's eight. So what's the problem?

FELIX   If you knew you were going to be late, why didn't you call me?

OSCAR   (*Pauses while making the knot in his tie*)   I couldn't call you. I was busy.

FELIX   Too busy to pick up a phone? Where were you?

OSCAR   I was in the office, working.

FELIX   Working? Ha!

OSCAR   Yes. Working!

FELIX   I called your office at seven o'clock. You were gone.

OSCAR   (*Tucking in his shirt*)   It took me an hour to get home. I couldn't get a cab.

FELIX   Since when do they have cabs in Hannigan's Bar?

OSCAR   Wait a minute. I want to get this down on a tape recorder, because no one'll believe me. You mean now I have to call you if I'm coming home late for dinner?

FELIX   (*Crosses to* OSCAR)   Not *any* dinner. Just the ones I've been slaving over since two o'clock this afternoon— to help save *you* money to pay your wife's alimony.

OSCAR   (*Controlling himself*)   Felix, this is no time to have a domestic quarrel. We have two girls coming down any minute.

FELIX   You mean you told them to be here at eight o'clock?

OSCAR   (*Takes his jacket and crosses to the couch, then sits and takes some dip from the coffee table*)   I don't remember what I said. Seven thirty, eight o'clock. What difference does it make?

FELIX   (*Follows* OSCAR)   I'll tell you what difference. You told me they were coming at seven thirty. You were

73

going to be here at seven to help me with the hors d'oeuvres. At seven thirty they arrive and we have cocktails. At eight o'clock we have dinner. It is now eight o'clock. *My London broil is finished!* If we don't eat now the whole damned thing'll be *dried out!*

OSCAR   Oh, God, help me.

FELIX   Never mind helping *you.* Tell Him to save the meat. Because we got nine dollars and thirty-four cents worth drying up in there right now.

OSCAR   Can't you keep it warm?

FELIX   (*Pacing*) What do you think I am, the Magic Chef? I'm lucky I got it to come out at eight o'clock. What am I going to do?

OSCAR   I don't know. Keep pouring gravy on it.

FELIX   What gravy?

OSCAR   Don't you have any gravy?

FELIX   (*Storms over to* OSCAR) Where the hell am I going to get gravy at eight o'clock?

OSCAR   (*Getting up*) I thought it comes when you cook the meat.

FELIX   (*Follows him*) When you *cook the meat?* You don't know the first thing you're talking about. You have to make gravy. It doesn't come!

OSCAR   You asked my advice, I'm giving it to you.
(*He puts on his jacket*)

FELIX   Advice? (*He waves the ladle in his face*) You didn't know where the kitchen was till I came here and showed you.

OSCAR   You wanna talk to me, put down the spoon.

74

FELIX (*Exploding in rage, again waving the ladle in his face*) Spoon? You dumb ignoramus. It's a ladle. You don't even know it's a ladle.

OSCAR All right, Felix, get a hold of yourself.

FELIX (*Pulls himself together and sits on the love seat*) You think it's so easy? Go on. The kitchen's all yours. Go make a London broil for four people who come a half hour late.

OSCAR (*To no one in particular*) Listen to me. I'm arguing with him over gravy.
(*The bell rings*)

FELIX (*Jumps up*) Well, they're here. Our dinner guests. I'll get a saw and cut the meat.
(*He starts for the kitchen*)

OSCAR (*Stopping him*) Stay where you are!

FELIX I'm not taking the blame for this dinner.

OSCAR Who's blaming you? Who even *cares* about the dinner?

FELIX (*Moves to* OSCAR) I care. I take *pride* in what I do. And you're going to explain to them exactly what happened.

OSCAR All right, you can take a Polaroid picture of me coming in at eight o'clock! Now take off that stupid apron because I'm opening the door.
(*He rips the towel off* FELIX *and goes to the door*)

FELIX (*Takes his jacket from a dining chair and puts it on*) I just want to get one thing clear. This is the last time I ever cook for you. Because people like you don't even appreciate a decent meal. That's why they have TV dinners.

OSCAR You through?

FELIX I'm through!

OSCAR Then smile. (OSCAR *smiles and opens the door. The girls poke their heads through the door. They are in their young thirties and somewhat attractive. They are undoubtedly British*) Well, hello.

GWENDOLYN (*To* OSCAR) Hallo!

CECILY (*To* OSCAR) Hallo.

GWENDOLYN I do hope we're not late.

OSCAR No, no. You timed it perfectly. Come on in. (*He points to them as they enter*) Er, Felix, I'd like you to meet two very good friends of mine, Gwendolyn and Cecily . . .

CECILY (*Pointing out his mistake*) Cecily and Gwendolyn.

OSCAR Oh, yes. Cecily and Gwendolyn . . . er (*Trying to remember their last name*) Er . . . Don't tell me. Robin? No, no. Cardinal?

GWENDOLYN Wrong both times. It's Pigeon!

OSCAR Pigeon. Right. Cecily and Gwendolyn Pigeon.

GWENDOLYN (*To* FELIX) You don't spell it like Walter Pidgeon. You spell it like "Coo-Coo" Pigeon.

OSCAR We'll remember that if it comes up. Cecily and Gwendolyn, I'd like you to meet my room-mate, and our chef for the evening, Felix Ungar.

CECILY (*Holding her hand out*) Heh d'yew dew?

FELIX (*Moving to her and shaking her hand*) How do you do?

GWENDOLYN (*Holding her hand out*) Heh d'yew dew?

FELIX (*Stepping up on the landing and shaking her hand*) How do you do you?

> (*This puts him nose to nose with* OSCAR, *and there is an awkward pause as they look at each other*)

OSCAR   Well, we did that beautifully. Why don't we sit down and make ourselves comfortable?

> (FELIX *steps aside and ushers the girls down into the room. There is ad libbing and a bit of confusion and milling about as they all squeeze between the armchair and the couch, and the* PIGEONS *finally seat themselves on the couch.* OSCAR *sits in the armchair, and* FELIX *sneaks past him to the love seat. Finally all have settled down*)

CECILY   This is ever so nice, isn't it, Gwen?

GWENDOLYN (*Looking around*)   Lovely. And much nicer than our flat. Do you have help?

OSCAR   Er, yes. I have a man who comes in every night.

CECILY   Aren't you the lucky one?

> (CECILY, GWENDOLYN *and* OSCAR *all laugh at her joke.* OSCAR *looks over at* FELIX *but there is no response*)

OSCAR (*Rubs his hands together*)   Well, isn't this nice? I was telling Felix yesterday about how we happened to meet.

GWENDOLYN   Oh? Who's Felix?

OSCAR (*A little embarrassed, he points to* FELIX)   He is!

GWENDOLYN   Oh, yes, of course. I'm so sorry.

> (FELIX *nods that it's all right*)

CECILY   You know it happened to us again this morning.

OSCAR   What did?

77

GWENDOLYN Stuck in the elevator again.

OSCAR Really? Just the two of you?

CECILY And poor old Mr. Kessler from the third floor. We were in there half an hour.

OSCAR No kidding? What happened?

GWENDOLYN Nothing much, I'm afraid.
(CECILY *and* GWENDOLYN *both laugh at her latest joke, joined by* OSCAR. *He once again looks over at* FELIX, *but there is no response*)

OSCAR (*Rubs his hands again*) Well, this really is nice.

CECILY And ever so much cooler than our place.

GWENDOLYN It's like equatorial Africa on our side of the building.

CECILY Last night it was so bad Gwen and I sat there in nature's own cooling ourselves in front of the open fridge. Can you imagine such a thing?

OSCAR Er, I'm working on it.

GWENDOLYN Actually, it's impossible to get a night's sleep. Cec and I really don't know what to do.

OSCAR Why don't you sleep with an air conditioner?

GWENDOLYN We haven't got one.

OSCAR I know. But we have.

GWENDOLYN Oh, you! I told you about that one, didn't I, Cec?

FELIX They say it may rain Friday.
(*They all stare at* FELIX)

GWENDOLYN Oh?

CECILY That should cool things off a bit.

78

OSCAR   I wouldn't be surprised.

FELIX   Although sometimes it gets hotter after it rains.

GWENDOLYN   Yes, it does, doesn't it?
   (*They continue to stare at* FELIX)

FELIX (*Jumps up and, picking up the ladle, starts for the kitchen*)   Dinner is served!

OSCAR (*Stopping him*)   No, it isn't!

FELIX   Yes, it is!

OSCAR   No, it isn't! I'm sure the girls would like a cocktail first. (*To the girls*) Wouldn't you, girls?

GWENDOLYN   Well, I wouldn't put up a struggle.

OSCAR   There you are. (*To* CECILY) What would you like?

CECILY   Oh, I really don't know. (*To* OSCAR) What have you got?

FELIX   London broil.

OSCAR (*To* FELIX)   She means to drink. (*To* CECILY) We have everything. And what we don't have, I mix in the medicine cabinet. What'll it be?
   (*He crouches next to her*)

CECILY   Oh, a double vodka.

GWENDOLYN   Cecily, not before dinner.

CECILY (*To the men*)   My sister. She watches over me like a mother hen. (*To* OSCAR) Make it a *small* double vodka.

OSCAR   A small double vodka! And for the beautiful mother hen?

GWENDOLYN   Oh, I'd like something cool. I think I would

like to have a double Drambuie with some crushed ice, unless you don't have the crushed ice.

OSCAR   I was up all night with a sledge hammer. I shall return!
        (*He goes to the bar and gets bottles of vodka and Drambuie*)

FELIX (*Going to him*)   Where are you going?

OSCAR   To get the refreshments.

FELIX (*Starting to panic*)   Inside? What'll *I* do?

OSCAR   You can finish the weather report.
        (*He exits into the kitchen*)

FELIX (*Calls after him*)   Don't forget to look at my meat!
        (*He turns and faces the girls. He crosses to a chair and sits. He crosses his legs nonchalantly. But he is ill at ease and he crosses them again. He is becoming aware of the silence and he can no longer get away with just smiling*) Er, Oscar tells me you're sisters.

CECILY   Yes. That's right.
        (*She looks at* GWENDOLYN)

FELIX   From England.

GWENDOLYN   Yes. That's right.
        (*She looks at* CECILY)

FELIX   I see. (*Silence. Then, his little joke*) We're not brothers.

CECILY   Yes. We know.

FELIX   Although I am a brother. I have a brother who's a doctor. He lives in Buffalo. That's upstate in New York.

GWENDOLYN (*Taking a cigarette from her purse*)   Yes, we know.

FELIX   You know my brother?

GWENDOLYN   No. We know that Buffalo is upstate in New York.

FELIX   Oh!
   (*He gets up, takes a cigarette lighter from the side table and moves to light* GWENDOLYN's *cigarette*)

CECILY   We've been there! Have you?

FELIX   No! Is it nice?

CECILY   Lovely.
   (FELIX *closes the lighter on* GWENDOLYN's *cigarette and turns to go back to his chair, taking the cigarette, now caught in the lighter, with him. He notices the cigarette and hastily gives it back to* GWENDOLYN, *stopping to light it once again. He puts the lighter back on the table and sits down nervously. There is a pause*)

FELIX   Isn't that interesting? How long have you been in the United States of America?

CECILY   Almost four years now.

FELIX (*Nods*)   Uh huh. Just visiting?

GWENDOLYN (*Looks at* CECILY)   No! We live here.

FELIX   And you work here too, do you?

CECILY   Yes. We're secretaries for Slenderama.

GWENDOLYN   You know. The health club.

CECILY   People bring us their bodies and we do wonderful things with them.

GWENDOLYN   Actually, if you're interested, we can get you ten per cent off.

CECILY   Off the price, not off your body.

FELIX   Yes, I see. (*He laughs. They all laugh. Suddenly he shouts toward the kitchen*) Oscar, where's the drinks?

OSCAR (*Offstage*)   Coming! Coming!

CECILY   What field of endeavor are you engaged in?

FELIX   I write the news for CBS.

CECILY   Oh! Fascinating!

GWENDOLYN   Where do you get your ideas from?

FELIX (*He looks at her as though she's a Martian*)   From the news.

GWENDOLYN   Oh, yes, of course. Silly me . . .

CECILY   Maybe you can mention Gwen and I in one of your news reports.

FELIX   Well, if you do something spectacular, maybe I will.

CECILY   Oh, we've done spectacular things but I don't think we'd want it spread all over the telly, do you, Gwen?
        (*They both laugh*)

FELIX (*He laughs too, then cries out almost for help*) Oscar!

OSCAR (*Offstage*)   Yeah, yeah!

FELIX (*To the girls*)   It's such a large apartment, sometimes you have to shout.

GWENDOLYN   Just you two baches live here?

FELIX   Baches? Oh, bachelors! We're not bachelors. We're divorced. That is, Oscar's divorced. I'm *getting* divorced.

CECILY   Oh. Small world. We've cut the dinghy loose too, as they say.

GWENDOLYN Well, you couldn't have a *better* matched foursome, could you?

FELIX (*Smiles weakly*) No, I suppose not.

GWENDOLYN Although technically I'm a widow. I was divorcing my husband, but he died before the final papers came through.

FELIX Oh, I'm awfully sorry. (*Sighs*) It's a terrible thing, isn't it? Divorce.

GWENDOLYN It can be—if you haven't got the right solicitor.

CECILY That's true. Sometimes they can drag it out for months. I was lucky. Snip, cut and I was free.

FELIX I mean it's terrible what it can do to people. After all, what is divorce? It's taking two happy people and tearing their lives completely apart. It's inhuman, don't you think so?

CECILY Yes, it can be an awful bother.

GWENDOLYN But of course, that's all water under the bridge now, eh? Ei, I'm terribly sorry, but I think I've forgotten your name.

FELIX Felix.

GWENDOLYN Oh, yes. Felix.

CECILY Like the cat.
        (FELIX *takes his wallet from his jacket pocket*)

GWENDOLYN Well, the Pigeons will have to beware of the cat, won't they?
        (*She laughs*)

CECILY (*Nibbles on a nut from the dish*) Mmm, cashews. Lovely.

FELIX (*Takes a snapshot out of his wallet*) This is the worst part of breaking up.
>   (*He hands the picture to* CECILY)

CECILY (*Looks at it*) Childhood sweethearts, were you?

FELIX No, no. That's my little boy and girl. (CECILY *gives the picture to* GWENDOLYN, *takes a pair of glasses from her purse and puts them on*) He's seven, she's five.

CECILY (*Looks again*) Oh! Sweet.

FELIX They live with their mother.

GWENDOLYN I imagine you must miss them terribly.

FELIX (*Takes back the picture and looks at it longingly*) I can't stand being away from them. (*Shrugs*) But— that's what happens with divorce.

CECILY When do you get to see them?

FELIX Every night. I stop there on my way home! Then I take them on the weekends, and I get them on holidays and July and August.

CECILY Oh! Well, when is it that you miss them?

FELIX Whenever I'm not there. If they didn't have to go to school so early, I'd go over and make them breakfast. They love my French toast.

GWENDOLYN You're certainly a devoted father.

FELIX It's Frances who's the wonderful one.

CECILY She's the little girl?

FELIX No. She's the mother. My wife.

GWENDOLYN The one you're divorcing?

FELIX (*Nods*) Mm! She's done a terrific job bringing them up. They always look so nice. They're so polite. Speak beautifully. Never, "Yeah." Always, "Yes."

They're such good kids. And she did it all. She's the kind of woman who— Ah, what am I saying? You don't want to hear any of this.

(*He puts the picture back in his wallet*)

CECILY Nonsense. You have a right to be proud. You have two beautiful children and a wonderful ex-wife.

FELIX (*Containing his emotions*) I know. I know. (*He hands* CECILY *another snapshot*) That's her. Frances.

GWENDOLYN (*Looking at the picture*) Oh, she's pretty. Isn't she pretty, Cecy?

CECILY Oh, yes. Pretty. A pretty girl. Very pretty.

FELIX (*Takes the picture back*) Thank you. (*Shows them another snapshot*) Isn't this nice?

GWENDOLYN (*Looks*) There's no one in the picture.

FELIX I know. It's a picture of our living room. We had a beautiful apartment.

GWENDOLYN Oh, yes. Pretty. Very pretty.

CECILY Those are lovely lamps.

FELIX Thank you! (*Takes the picture*) We bought them in Mexico on our honeymoon. (*He looks at the picture again*) I used to love to come home at night. (*He's beginning to break*) That was my whole life. My wife, my kids—and my apartment.

(*He breaks down and sobs*)

CECILY Does she have the lamps now too?

FELIX (*Nods*) I gave her everything. It'll never be like that again. Never! I—I— (*He turns his head away*) I'm sorry. (*He takes out a handkerchief and dabs his eyes.* GWENDOLYN *and* CECILY *look at each other with compassion*) Please forgive me. I didn't mean to get emo-

85

tional. (*Trying to pull himself together, he picks up a bowl from the side table and offers it to the girls*) Would you like some potato chips?

    (CECILY *takes the bowl*)

GWENDOLYN   You mustn't be ashamed. I think it's a rare quality in a man to be able to cry.

FELIX   (*Puts a hand over his eyes*)   Please. Let's not talk about it.

CECILY   I think it's sweet. Terribly, terribly sweet.

    (*She takes a potato chip*)

FELIX   You're just making it worse.

GWENDOLYN   (*Teary-eyed*)   It's so refreshing to hear a man speak so highly of the woman he's divorcing! Oh, dear. (*She takes out her handkerchief*) Now you've got me thinking about poor Sydney.

CECILY   Oh, Gwen. Please don't.

    (*She puts the bowl down*)

GWENDOLYN   It was a good marriage at first. Everyone said so. Didn't they, Cecily? Not like you and George.

CECILY   (*The past returns as she comforts* GWENDOLYN) That's right. George and I were never happy. Not for one single, solitary day.

    (*She remembers her unhappiness, grabs her handkerchief and dabs her eyes. All three are now sitting with handkerchiefs at their eyes*)

FELIX   Isn't this ridiculous?

GWENDOLYN   I don't know what brought this on. I was feeling so good a few minutes ago.

CECILY   I haven't cried since I was fourteen.

86

FELIX   Just let it pour out. It'll make you feel much better.
I always do.

GWENDOLYN   Oh, dear; oh, dear; oh, dear.
    (*All three sit sobbing into their handkerchiefs.
    Suddenly* OSCAR *bursts happily into the room with
    a tray full of drinks. He is all smiles*)

OSCAR (*Like a corny M.C.*)   Is ev-rybuddy happy? (*Then
he sees the maudlin scene.* FELIX *and the girls quickly
try to pull themselves together*) What the hell happened?

FELIX   Nothing! Nothing!
    (*He quickly puts his handkerchief away*)

OSCAR   What do you mean, nothing? I'm gone three minutes and I walk into a funeral parlor. What did you say
to them?

FELIX   I didn't say anything. Don't start in again, Oscar.

OSCAR   I can't leave you alone for five seconds. Well, if
you really want to cry, go inside and look at your London
broil.

FELIX (*He rushes madly into the kitchen*)   Oh, my gosh!
Why didn't you call me? I told you to call me.

OSCAR (*Giving a drink to* CECILY)   I'm sorry, girls. I forgot to warn you about Felix. He's a walking soap opera.

GWENDOLYN   I think he's the dearest thing I ever met.

CECILY (*Taking the glass*)   He's so sensitive. So fragile. I
just want to bundle him up in my arms and take care of
him.

OSCAR (*Holds out* GWENDOLYN's *drink. At this, he puts it
back down on the tray and takes a swallow from his own
drink*)   Well, I think when he comes out of that kitchen
you may have to.
    (*Sure enough,* FELIX *comes out of the kitchen onto*

the landing looking like a wounded puppy. With a protective kitchen glove, he holds a pan with the exposed London broil. Black is the color of his true love)

FELIX *(Very calmly)* I'm going down to the delicatessen. I'll be right back.

OSCAR *(Going to him)* Wait a minute. Maybe it's not so bad. Let's see it.

FELIX *(Shows him)* Here! Look! Nine dollars and thirty-four cents worth of ashes! *(Pulls the pan away. To the girls)* I'll get some corned beef sandwiches.

OSCAR *(Trying to get a look at it)* Give it to me! Maybe we can save some of it.

FELIX *(Holding it away from OSCAR)* There's nothing to save. It's all black meat. Nobody likes black meat!

OSCAR Can't I even look at it?

FELIX No, you can't look at it!

OSCAR Why can't I look at it?

FELIX If you looked at your watch before, you wouldn't have to look at the black meat now! Leave it alone! *(He turns to go back into the kitchen)*

GWENDOLYN *(Going to him)* Felix! Can we look at it?

CECILY *(Turning to him, kneeling on the couch)* Please? *(FELIX stops in the kitchen doorway. He hesitates for a moment. He likes them. Then he turns and wordlessly holds the pan out to them. GWENDOLYN and CECILY inspect it wordlessly, and then turn away sobbing quietly. To OSCAR)* How about Chinese food?

OSCAR A wonderful idea.

GWENDOLYN I've got a better idea. Why don't we just make pot luck in the kitchen?

OSCAR A *much* better idea.

FELIX I used up all the pots!
(He crosses to the love seat and sits, still holding the pan)

CECILY Well, then we can eat up in *our* place. We have tons of Horn and Hardart's.

OSCAR *(Gleefully)* That's the best idea I ever heard.

GWENDOLYN Of course it's awfully hot up there. You'll have to take off your jackets.

OSCAR *(Smiling)* We can always open up a refrigerator.

CECILY *(Gets her purse from the couch)* Give us five minutes to get into our cooking things.
(GWENDOLYN gets her purse from the couch)

OSCAR Can't you make it four? I'm suddenly starving to death.
(The girls are crossing to the door)

GWENDOLYN Don't forget the wine.

OSCAR How could I forget the wine?

CECILY And a corkscrew.

OSCAR *And* a corkscrew.

GWENDOLYN And Felix.

OSCAR No, I won't forget Felix.

CECILY Ta, ta!

OSCAR Ta, ta!

GWENDOLYN Ta, ta!
(The girls exit)

OSCAR (*Throws a kiss at the closed door*) You bet your sweet little crumpets, "Ta, Ta!" (*He wheels around beaming and quickly gathers up the corkscrew from the bar, and picks up the wine and the records*) Felix, I love you. You've just overcooked us into one hell of a night. Come on, get the ice bucket. Ready or not, here we come.

(*He runs to the door*)

FELIX (*Sitting motionless*) I'm not going!

OSCAR What?

FELIX I said I'm not going.

OSCAR (*Crossing to* FELIX) Are you out of your mind? Do you know what's waiting for us up there? You've just been invited to spend the evening in a two-bedroom hot-house with the Coo-Coo Pigeon Sisters! What do you mean you're not going?

FELIX I don't know how to talk to them. I don't know what to say. I already told them about my brother in Buffalo. I've used up my conversation.

OSCAR Felix, they're crazy about you. They told me! One of them wants to wrap you up and make a bundle out of you. You're doing better than I am! Get the ice bucket.

(*He starts for the door*)

FELIX Don't you understand? I cried! I cried in front of two women.

OSCAR (*Stops*) And they *loved* it! I'm thinking of getting hysterical. (*Goes to the door*) Will you get the ice bucket?

FELIX But why did I cry? Because I felt guilty. Emotion-ally I'm still tied to Frances and the kids.

OSCAR Well, untie the knot just for tonight, will you!

FELIX I don't want to discuss it any more. (*Starts for the kitchen*) I'm going to scrub the pots and wash my hair. (*He goes into the kitchen and puts the pan in the sink*)

OSCAR (*Yelling*) Your greasy pots and your greasy hair can wait. You're coming upstairs with me!

FELIX (*In the kitchen*) I'm not! *I'm not!*

OSCAR What am I going to do with two girls? Felix, don't do this to me. I'll never forgive you!

FELIX I'm not going!

OSCAR (*Screams*) All right, damn you, I'll go without you! (*And he storms out the door and slams it. Then it opens and he comes in again*) Are you coming?

FELIX (*Comes out of the kitchen looking at a magazine*) No.

OSCAR You mean you're not going to make any effort to change? This is the person you're going to be—until the day you die?

FELIX (*Sitting on the couch*) We are what we are.

OSCAR (*Nods, then crosses to a window, pulls back the drapes and opens the window wide. Then he starts back to the door*) It's twelve floors, not eleven.

(*He walks out as* FELIX *stares at the open windows*)

Curtain

Act Three

The next evening about 7:30 P.M. The room is once again set up for the poker game, with the dining table pulled down, the chairs set about it, and the love seat moved back beneath the windows in the alcove. FELIX *appears from the bedroom with a vacuum cleaner. He is doing a thorough job on the rug. As he vacuums around the table, the door opens and* OSCAR *comes in wearing a summer hat and carrying a newspaper. He glares at* FELIX, *who is still vacuuming, and shakes his head contemptuously. He crosses behind* FELIX, *leaving his hat on the side table next to the armchair, and goes into his bedroom.* FELIX *is not aware of his presence. Then suddenly the power stops on the vacuum, as* OSCAR *has obviously pulled the plug in the bedroom.* FELIX *tries switching the button on and off a few times, then turns to go back into the bedroom. He stops and realizes what's happened as* OSCAR *comes back into the room.* OSCAR *takes a cigar out of his pocket and as he crosses in front of* FELIX *to the couch, he unwraps it and drops the wrappings carelessly on the floor. He then steps up on the couch and walks back and forth mashing down the pillows. Stepping down, he plants one foot on the armchair and then sits on the couch, taking a wooden match from the coffee table and striking it on the table to light his cigar. He flips the used match onto the rug and settles*

95

back to read his newspaper. FELIX *has watched this all in silence, and now carefully picks up the cigar wrappings and the match and drops them into* OSCAR's *hat. He then dusts his hands and takes the vacuum cleaner into the kitchen, pulling the cord in after him.* OSCAR *takes the wrappings from the hat and puts them in the butt-filled ashtray on the coffee table. Then he takes the ashtray and dumps it on the floor. As he once more settles down with his newspaper,* FELIX *comes out of the kitchen carrying a tray with a steaming dish of spaghetti. As he crosses behind* OSCAR *to the table, he indicates that it smells delicious and passes it close to* OSCAR *to make sure* OSCAR *smells the fantastic dish he's missing. As* FELIX *sits and begins to eat,* OSCAR *takes a can of aerosol spray from the bar, and circling the table, sprays all around* FELIX, *then puts the can down next to him and goes back to his newspaper.*

FELIX (*Pushing the spaghetti away*)   All right, how much longer is this gonna go on?

OSCAR (*Reading his paper*)   Are you talking to me?

FELIX   That's right, I'm talking to you.

OSCAR   What do you want to know?

FELIX   I want to know if you're going to spend the rest of your life not talking to me. Because if you are, I'm going to buy a radio. (*No reply*) Well? (*No reply*) I see. You're not going to talk to me. (*No reply*) All right. Two can play at this game. (*Pause*) If you're not going to talk to me, I'm not going to talk to you. (*No reply*) I can act childish too, you know. (*No reply*) I can go on without talking just as long as you can.

OSCAR   Then why the hell don't you shut up?

FELIX   Are you talking to me?

OSCAR You had your chance to talk last night. I begged you to come upstairs with me. From now on I never want to hear a word from that shampooed head as long as you live. That's a warning, Felix.

FELIX (*Stares at him*) I stand warned. Over and out!

OSCAR (*Gets up, takes a key out of his pocket and slams it on the table*) There's a key to the back door. If you stick to the hallway and your room, you won't get hurt.
(*He sits back down on the couch*)

FELIX I don't think I gather the entire meaning of that remark.

OSCAR Then I'll explain it to you. Stay out of my way.

FELIX (*Picks up the key and moves to the couch*) I think you're serious. I think you're really serious. Are you serious?

OSCAR This is my apartment. Everything in my apartment is mine. The only thing here that's yours is you. Just stay in your room and speak softly.

FELIX Yeah, you're serious. Well, let me remind you that I pay half the rent and I'll go into any room I want.
(*He gets up angrily and starts toward the hallway*)

OSCAR Where are you going?

FELIX I'm going to walk around your bedroom.

OSCAR (*Slams down his newspaper*) You stay out of there.

FELIX (*Steaming*) Don't tell me where to go. I pay a hundred and twenty dollars a month.

OSCAR That was off-season. Starting tomorrow the rates are twelve dollars a day.

FELIX All right. (*He takes some bills out of his pocket

and slams them down on the table) There you are. I'm paid up for today. Now I'm going to walk in your bedroom.

(He starts to storm off)

OSCAR   Stay out of there! Stay out of my room!
(He chases after him. FELIX *dodges around the table as* OSCAR *blocks the hallway)*

FELIX *(Backing away, keeping the table between them)* Watch yourself! Just watch yourself, Oscar!

OSCAR *(With a pointing finger)* I'm warning you. You want to live here, I don't want to see you, I don't want to hear you and I don't want to smell your cooking. Now get this spaghetti off my poker table.

FELIX   Ha! Ha, ha!

OSCAR   What the hell's so funny?

FELIX   It's not spaghetti. It's linguini!
*(*OSCAR *picks up the plate of linguini, crosses to the doorway and hurls it into the kitchen)*

OSCAR   Now it's garbage!
(He paces by the couch)

FELIX *(Looks at* OSCAR *unbelievingly: what an insane thing to do)* You are crazy! I'm a neurotic nut but *you* are crazy!

OSCAR   *I'm* crazy, heh? That's really funny coming from a fruitcake like you.

FELIX *(Goes to the kitchen door and looks in at the mess. Turns back to* OSCAR*)* I'm not cleaning that up.

OSCAR   Is that a promise?

FELIX   Did you hear what I said? I'm not cleaning it up.

It's your mess. (*Looking into the kitchen again*) Look at it. Hanging all over the walls.

OSCAR (*Crosses to the landing and looks in the kitchen door*) I like it.
(*He closes the door and paces around*)

FELIX (*Fumes*) You'd just let it lie there, wouldn't you? Until it turns hard and brown and . . . Yich, it's disgusting. I'm cleaning it up.
(*He goes into the kitchen.* OSCAR *chases after him. There is the sound of a struggle and falling pots*)

OSCAR *Leave it alone!* You touch one strand of that linguini—and I'm gonna punch you right in your sinuses.

FELIX (*Dashes out of the kitchen with* OSCAR *in pursuit. He stops and tries to calm* OSCAR *down*) Oscar, I'd like you to take a couple of phenobarbital.

OSCAR (*Points*) Go to your room! Did you hear what I said? *Go to your room!*

FELIX All right, let's everybody just settle down, heh?
(*He puts his hand on* OSCAR's *shoulder to calm him but* OSCAR *pulls away violently from his touch*)

OSCAR If you want to live through this night, you'd better tie me up and lock your doors and windows.

FELIX (*Sits at the table with a great pretense of calm*) All right, Oscar, I'd like to know what's happened?

OSCAR (*Moves toward him*) What's *happened?*

FELIX (*Hurriedly slides over to the next chair*) That's right. Something must have caused you to go off the deep end like this. What is it? Something I said? Something I did? Heh? What?

OSCAR (*Pacing*) It's nothing you said. It's nothing you did. It's *you!*

FELIX I see. Well, that's plain enough.

OSCAR I could make it plainer but I don't want to hurt you.

FELIX What is it, the cooking? The cleaning? The crying?

OSCAR (*Moving toward him*) I'll tell you exactly what it is. It's the cooking, cleaning and crying. It's the talking in your sleep, it's the moose calls that open your ears at two o'clock in the morning. I can't take it any more, Felix. I'm crackin' up. Everything you do irritates me. And when you're not here, the things I know you're gonna do when you come in irritate me. You leave me little notes on my pillow. I told you a hundred times, I can't stand little notes on my pillow. "We're all out of Corn Flakes. F.U." It took me three hours to figure out that F.U. was Felix Ungar. It's not your fault, Felix. It's a rotten combination.

FELIX I get the picture.

OSCAR That's just the frame. The picture I haven't even painted yet. I got a typewritten list in my office of the "Ten Most Aggravating Things You Do That Drive Me Berserk." But last night was the topper. Oh, that was the topper. Oh, that was the ever-loving lulu of all times.

FELIX What are you talking about, the London broil?

OSCAR No, not the London broil. I'm talking about those two lamb chops. (*He points upstairs*) I had it all set up with that English Betty Boop and her sister, and I wind up drinking tea all night and telling them *your* life story.

FELIX (*Jumps up*) Oho! So *that's* what's bothering you. That I loused up your evening!

OSCAR After the mood you put them in, I'm surprised they didn't go out to Rockaway and swim back to England.

FELIX Don't blame me. I warned you not to make the date in the first place.
(*He makes his point by shaking his finger in* OS-CAR's *face*)

OSCAR Don't point that finger at me unless you intend to use it!

FELIX (*Moves in nose to nose with* OSCAR) All right, Oscar, get off my back. Get off! Off!
(*Startled by his own actions,* FELIX *jumps back from* OSCAR, *warily circles him, crosses to the couch and sits*)

OSCAR What's this? A display of temper? I haven't seen you really angry since the day I dropped my cigar in your pancake batter.
(*He starts toward the hallway*)

FELIX (*Threateningly*) Oscar, you're asking to hear something I don't want to say. But if I say it, I think you'd better hear it.

OSCAR (*Comes back to the table, places both hands on it and leans toward* FELIX) If you've got anything on your chest besides your chin, you'd better get it off.

FELIX (*Strides to the table, places both hands on it and leans toward* OSCAR. *They are nose to nose*) All right, I warned you. You're a wonderful guy, Oscar. You've done everything for me. If it weren't for you, I don't know what would have happened to me. You took me in here, gave me a place to live and something to live for. I'll never forget you for that. You're tops with me, Oscar.

OSCAR (*Motionless*) If I've just been told off, I think I may have missed it.

FELIX It's coming now! You're also one of the biggest slobs in the world.

OSCAR I see.

FELIX And completely unreliable.

OSCAR Finished?

FELIX Undependable.

OSCAR Is that it?

FELIX And irresponsible.

OSCAR Keep going. I think you're hot.

FELIX That's it. I'm finished. *Now* you've been told off. How do you like that?
(*He crosses to the couch*)

OSCAR (*Straightening up*) Good. Because now I'm going to tell *you* off. For six months I lived alone in this apartment. All alone in eight rooms. I was dejected, despondent and disgusted. Then *you* moved in—my dearest and closest friend. And after three weeks of close, personal contact—I am about to have a nervous breakdown! Do me a favor. Move into the kitchen. Live with your pots, your pans, your ladle and your meat thermometer. When you want to come out, ring a bell and I'll run into the bedroom. (*Almost breaking down*) I'm asking you nicely, Felix—as a friend. Stay out of my way!
(*And he goes into the bedroom*)

FELIX (*Is hurt by this, then remembers something. He calls after him*) Walk on the paper, will you? The floors are wet. (OSCAR *comes out of the door. He is glaring maniacally, as he slowly strides back down the hallway.* FELIX *quickly puts the couch between him and* OSCAR) Awright, keep away. Keep away from me.

OSCAR (*Chasing him around the couch*) Come on. Let me get in one shot. You pick it. Head, stomach or kidneys.

FELIX (*Dodging about the room*) You're gonna find yourself in one sweet law suit, Oscar.

OSCAR It's no use running, Felix. There's only eight rooms and I know the short cuts.
> (*They are now poised at opposite ends of the couch.* FELIX *picks up a lamp for protection*)

FELIX Is this how you settle your problems, Oscar? Like an animal?

OSCAR All right. You wanna see how I settle my problems. I'll show you. (*Storms off into* FELIX's *bedroom. There is the sound of falling objects and he returns with a suitcase*) I'll show you how I settle them. (*Throws the suitcase on the table*) There! That's how I settle them!

FELIX (*Bewildered, looks at the suitcase*) Where are you going?

OSCAR (*Exploding*) Not me, you idiot! You. You're the one who's going. I want you out of here. Now! Tonight!
> (*He opens the suitcase*)

FELIX What are you talking about?

OSCAR It's all over, Felix. The whole marriage. We're getting an annulment! Don't you understand? I don't want to live with you any more. I want you to pack your things, tie it up with your Saran Wrap and get out of here.

FELIX You mean actually move out?

OSCAR   Actually, physically and immediately. I don't care where you go. Move into the Museum of Natural History. (*Goes into the kitchen. There is the crash of falling pots and pans*) I'm sure you'll be very comfortable there. You can dust around the Egyptian mummies to your heart's content. But I'm a human, living person. (*Comes out with a stack of cooking utensils which he throws into the open suitcase*) All I want is my freedom. Is that too much to ask for? (*Closes it*) There, you're all packed.

FELIX   You know, I've got a good mind to really leave.

OSCAR   (*Looking to the heavens*)   Why doesn't he ever listen to what I say? Why doesn't he hear me? I know I'm talking—I recognize my voice.

FELIX   (*Indignantly*)   Because if you really want me to go, I'll go.

OSCAR   Then go. I want you to go, so go. When are you going?

FELIX   When am I going, huh? Boy, you're in a bigger hurry than Frances was.

OSCAR   Take as much time as she gave you. I want you to follow your usual routine.

FELIX   In other words, you're throwing me out.

OSCAR   Not in other words. Those are the perfect ones. (*Picks up the suitcase and holds it out to* FELIX) I am throwing you out.

FELIX   All right, I just wanted to get the record straight. Let it be on *your* conscience.
        (*He goes into his bedroom*)

OSCAR   What? What? (*Follows him to the bedroom doorway*) Let what be on my conscience?

FELIX (*Comes out putting on his jacket and passes by* OS-CAR) That you're throwing me out. (*Stops and turns back to him*) I'm perfectly willing to stay and clear the air of our differences. But you refuse, right?

OSCAR (*Still holding the suitcase*) Right! I'm sick and tired of you clearing the air. That's why I want you to leave!

FELIX Okay, as long as I heard you say the words, "Get out of the house." Fine. But remember, what happens to me is your responsibility. Let it be on *your* head.
 (*He crosses to the door*)

OSCAR (*Follows him to the door and screams*) Wait a minute, damn it! Why can't you be thrown out like a decent human being? Why do you have to say things like, "Let it be on your head"? I don't want it on my head. I just want you out of the house.

FELIX What's the matter, Oscar? Can't cope with a little guilt feelings?

OSCAR (*Pounding the railing in frustration*) Damn you. I've been looking forward to throwing you out all day long, and now you even take the pleasure out of that.

FELIX Forgive me for spoiling your fun. I'm leaving now—according to your wishes and desires.
 (*He starts to open the door*)

OSCAR (*Pushes by* FELIX *and slams the door shut. He stands between* FELIX *and the door*) You're not leaving here until you take it back.

FELIX Take what back?

OSCAR "Let it be on your head." What the hell is that, the Curse of the Cat People?

FELIX Get out of my way, please.

OSCAR   Is this how you left that night with Frances? No wonder she wanted to have the room repainted right away. (*Points to* FELIX's *bedroom*) I'm gonna have yours dipped in bronze.

FELIX (*Sits on the back of the couch with his back to* OSCAR)   How can I leave if you're blocking the door?

OSCAR (*Very calmly*)   Felix, we've been friends a long time. For the sake of that friendship, please say, "Oscar, we can't stand each other; let's break up."

FELIX   I'll let you know what to do about my clothes. Either I'll call—or someone else will. (*Controlling great emotion*) I'd like to leave now.

(OSCAR, *resigned, moves out of the way.* FELIX *opens the door*)

OSCAR   Where will you go?

FELIX (*Turns in the doorway and looks at him*)   Where? (*He smiles*) Oh, come on, Oscar. You're not really interested, are you?

(*He exits.* OSCAR *looks as though he's about to burst with frustration. He calls after* FELIX)

OSCAR   All right, Felix, you win. (*Goes out into the hall*) We'll try to iron it out. Anything you want. Come back, Felix. Felix? *Felix?* Don't leave me like this—you louse! (*But* FELIX *is gone.* OSCAR *comes back into the room closing the door. He is limp. He searches for something to ease his enormous frustration. He throws a pillow at the door, and then paces about like a caged lion*) All right, Oscar, get a hold of yourself! He's gone! Keep saying that over and over. He's gone. He's really gone! (*He holds his head in pain*) He did it. He put a curse on me. It's on my head. I don't know what it is, but something's on my head. (*The doorbell rings and he looks up hopefully*) Please let it be him. Let it be Felix. Please give me one more chance to kill him.

(*Putting the suitcase on the sofa, he rushes to the door and opens it.* MURRAY *comes in with* VINNIE)

MURRAY (*Putting his jacket on a chair at the table*) Hey, what's the matter with Felix? He walked right by me with that "human sacrifice" look on his face again.

(*He takes off his shoes*)

VINNIE (*Laying his jacket on the love seat*) What's with him? I asked him where he's going and he said, "Only Oscar knows. Only Oscar knows." Where's he going, Oscar?

OSCAR (*Sitting at the table*) How the hell should I know? All right, let's get the game started, heh? Come on, get your chips.

MURRAY I have to get something to eat. I'm starving. Mmm, I think I smell spaghetti.

(*He goes into the kitchen*)

VINNIE Isn't he playing tonight?

(*He takes two chairs from the dining alcove and puts them at the table*)

OSCAR I don't want to discuss it. I don't even want to hear his name.

VINNIE Who? Felix?

OSCAR I told you not to mention his name.

VINNIE I didn't know what name you meant.

(*He clears the table and places what's left of* FELIX's *dinner on the bookcase*)

MURRAY (*Comes out of the kitchen*) Hey, did you know there's spaghetti all over the kitchen?

OSCAR Yes, I know, and it's not spaghetti; it's linguini.

MURRAY Oh. I thought it was spaghetti.
(*He goes back into the kitchen*)

VINNIE (*Taking the poker stuff from the bookcase and putting it on the table*) Why shouldn't I mention his name?

OSCAR Who?

VINNIE Felix. What's happened? Has something happened?
(SPEED *and* ROY *come in the open door*)

SPEED Yeah, what's the matter with Felix?
(SPEED *puts his jacket over a chair at the table.* ROY *sits in the armchair.* MURRAY *comes out of the kitchen with a six-pack of beer and bags of pretzels and chips. They all stare at* OSCAR *waiting for an answer. There is a long pause and then he stands up*)

OSCAR We broke up! I kicked him out. It was my decision. I threw him out of the house. All right? I admit it. Let it be on my head.

VINNIE Let what be on your head?

OSCAR How should I know? *Felix put it there!* Ask him!
(*He paces around to the right*)

MURRAY He'll go to pieces. I know Felix. He's gonna try something crazy.

OSCAR (*Turns to the boys*) Why do you think I did it?
(MURRAY *makes a gesture of disbelief and moves to the couch, putting down the beer and the bags.* OSCAR *moves to him*) You think I'm just selfish? That I wanted to be cruel? I did it for you—I did it for all of us.

ROY What are you talking about?

OSCAR (*Crosses to* ROY) All right, we've all been through the napkins and the ashtrays and the bacon, lettuce and tomato sandwiches. But that was just the beginning. Just the beginning. Do you know what he was planning for next Friday night's poker game? As a change of pace. Do you have any idea?

VINNIE What?

OSCAR A Luau! An Hawaiian Luau! Spareribs, roast pork and fried rice. They don't play poker like that in Honolulu.

MURRAY One thing has nothing to do with the other. We all know he's impossible, but he's still our friend, and he's still out on the street, and I'm still worried about him.

OSCAR (*Going to* MURRAY) And I'm not, heh? I'm not concerned? I'm not worried? Who do you think sent him out there in the first place?

MURRAY Frances!

OSCAR What?

MURRAY Frances sent him out in the first place. *You* sent him out in the second place. And whoever he lives with next will send him out in the third place. Don't you understand? It's Felix. He does it to himself.

OSCAR Why?

MURRAY I don't know why. *He* doesn't know why. There are people like that. There's a whole tribe in Africa who hit themselves on the head all day long.
(*He sums it all up with an eloquent gesture of resignation*)

OSCAR (*A slow realization of a whole new reason to be angry*) I'm not going to worry about him. Why should I? He's not worrying about me. He's somewhere out on the streets sulking and crying and having a wonderful time. If he had a spark of human decency he would leave us all alone and go back to Blanche.
(*He sits down at the table*)

VINNIE Why should he?

OSCAR (*Picks up a deck of cards*) Because it's his wife.

VINNIE No, Blanche is your wife. His wife is Frances.

OSCAR (*Stares at him*) What are you, some kind of wise guy?

VINNIE What did I say?

OSCAR (*Throws the cards in the air*) All right, the poker game is over. I don't want to play any more.
(*He paces around on the right*)

SPEED Who's playing? We didn't even start.

OSCAR (*Turns on him*) Is that all you can do is complain? Have you given one single thought to where Felix might be?

SPEED I thought you said you're not worried about him.

OSCAR (*Screams*) I'm not worried, damn it! I'm not worried. (*The doorbell rings. A gleeful look passes over* OSCAR's *face*) It's him. I bet it's him! (*The boys start to go for the door.* OSCAR *stops them*) Don't let him in; he's not welcome in this house.

MURRAY (*Moves toward the door*) Oscar, don't be childish. We've got to let him in.

OSCAR (*Stopping him and leading him to the table*) I won't give him the satisfaction of knowing we've been worrying about him. Sit down. Play cards. Like nothing happened.

MURRAY But, Oscar . . .

OSCAR Sit down. Everybody. Come on, sit down and play poker.
        (*They sit and* SPEED *begins to deal out cards*)

VINNIE (*Crossing to the door*) Oscar . . .

OSCAR All right, Vinnie, open the door.
        (VINNIE *opens the door. It is* GWENDOLYN *standing there*)

VINNIE (*Surprised*) Oh, hello. (*To* OSCAR) It's not him, Oscar.

GWENDOLYN How do you do.
        (*She walks into the room*)

OSCAR (*Crosses to her*) Oh, hello, Cecily. Boys, I'd like you to meet Cecily Pigeon.

GWENDOLYN Gwendolyn Pigeon. Please don't get up. (*To* OSCAR) May I see you for a moment, Mr. Madison?

OSCAR Certainly, Gwen. What's the matter?

GWENDOLYN I think you know. I've come for Felix's things.
        (OSCAR *looks at her in shock and disbelief. He looks at the boys, then back at* GWENDOLYN)

OSCAR Felix? My Felix?

GWENDOLYN Yes. Felix Ungar. That sweet, tortured man who's in my flat at this moment pouring his heart out to my sister.

OSCAR (*Turns to the boys*) You hear? I'm worried to death and he's up there getting tea and sympathy.

(CECILY *rushes in dragging a reluctant* FELIX *with her*)

CECILY   Gwen, Felix doesn't want to stay. Please tell him to stay.

FELIX   Really, girls, this is very embarrassing. I can go to a hotel. (*To the boys*) Hello, fellas.

GWENDOLYN   (*Overriding his objections*) Nonsense. I told you, we've plenty of room, and it's a very comfortable sofa. Isn't it, Cecy?

CECILY   (*Joining in*) Enormous. And we've rented an air conditioner.

GWENDOLYN   And we just don't like the idea of you wandering the streets looking for a place to live.

FELIX   But I'd be in the way. Wouldn't I be in the way?

GWENDOLYN   How could you possibly be in anyone's way?

OSCAR   You want to see a typewritten list?

GWENDOLYN   (*Turning on him*) Haven't you said enough already, Mr. Madison? (*To* FELIX) I won't take no for an answer. Just for a few days, Felix.

CECILY   Until you get settled.

GWENDOLYN   Please. Please say, "Yes," Felix.

CECILY   Oh, please—we'd be so happy.

FELIX (*Considers*)   Well, maybe just for a few days.

GWENDOLYN (*Jumping with joy*)   Oh, wonderful.

CECILY (*Ecstatic*)   Marvelous!

GWENDOLYN (*Crosses to the door*)   You get your things and come right up.

CECILY And come hungry. We're making dinner.

GWENDOLYN (*To the boys*) Good night, gentlemen; sorry to interrupt your bridge game.

CECILY (*To* FELIX) If you'd like, you can invite your friends to play in our flat.

GWENDOLYN (*To* FELIX) Don't be late. Cocktails in fifteen minutes.

FELIX I won't.

GWENDOLYN Ta, ta.

CECILY Ta, ta.

FELIX Ta, ta.
(*The girls leave.* FELIX *turns and looks at the fellows and smiles as he crosses the room into the bedroom. The five men stare dumbfounded at the door without moving. Finally* MURRAY *crosses to the door*)

SPEED (*To the others*) I told you. It's always the quiet guys.

MURRAY Gee, what nice girls.
(*He closes the door.* FELIX *comes out of the bedroom carrying two suits in a plastic cleaner's bag*)

ROY Hey, Felix, are you really gonna move in with them?

FELIX (*Turns back to them*) Just for a few days. Until I find my own place. Well, so long, fellows. You can drop your crumbs on the rug again.
(*He starts toward the door*)

OSCAR Hey, Felix. Aren't you going to thank me?

FELIX (*Stopping on the landing*) For what?

OSCAR For the two greatest things I ever did for you. Taking you in and throwing you out.

FELIX (*Lays his suits over the railing and goes to* OSCAR) You're right, Oscar. Thanks a lot. Getting kicked out twice is enough for any man. In gratitude, I remove the curse.

OSCAR (*Smiles*) Oh, bless you and thank you, Wicked Witch of the North.
(*They shake hands. The phone rings*)

FELIX Ah, that must be the girls.

MURRAY (*Picking up the phone*) Hello?

FELIX They hate it so when I'm late for cocktails. (*Turning to the boys*) Well, so long.

MURRAY It's your wife.

FELIX (*Turning to* MURRAY) Oh? Well, do me a favor, Murray. Tell her I can't speak to her now. But tell her I'll be calling her in a few days, because she and I have a lot to talk about. And tell her if I sound different to her, it's because I'm not the same man she kicked out three weeks ago. Tell her, Murray; tell her.

MURRAY I will when I see her. This is Oscar's wife.

FELIX Oh!

MURRAY (*Into the phone*) Just a minute, Blanche.
(OSCAR *crosses to the phone and sits on the arm of the couch*)

FELIX Well, so long, fellows.
(*He shakes hands with the boys, takes his suits and moves to the door*)

OSCAR (*Into the phone*) Hello? Yeah, Blanche. I got a pretty good idea why you're calling. You got my checks, right? Good. (FELIX *stops at the door, caught by* OSCAR's *conversation. He slowly comes back into the room to listen, putting his suits on the railing, and sitting down on the arm of the armchair*) So now I'm all paid up. No, no, I didn't win at the track. I've just been able to save a little money. I've been eating home a lot. (*Takes a pillow from the couch and throws it at* FELIX) Listen, Blanche, you don't have to thank me. I'm just doing what's right. Well, that's nice of you too. The apartment? No, I think you'd be shocked. It's in surprisingly good shape. (FELIX *throws the pillow back at* OSCAR) Say, Blanche, did Brucey get the goldfish I sent him? Yeah, well, I'll speak to you again soon, huh? Whenever you want. I don't go out much any more.

FELIX (*Gets up, takes his suits from the railing and goes to the door*) Well, good night, Mr. Madison. If you need me again, I get a dollar-fifty an hour.

OSCAR (*Makes a gesture to stop* FELIX *as he talks on the phone*) Well, kiss the kids for me. Good night, Blanche. (*Hangs up and turns to* FELIX) Felix?

FELIX (*At the opened door*) Yeah?

OSCAR How about next Friday night? You're not going to break up the game, are you?

FELIX Me? Never! Marriages may come and go, but the game must go on. So long, Frances.
(*He exits, closing the door*)

OSCAR (*Yelling after him*) So long, Blanche. (*The boys all look at* OSCAR *a moment*) All right, are we just gonna sit around or are we gonna play poker?

ROY We're gonna play poker.
(*There is a general hubbub as they pass out the beer, deal the cards and settle around the table*)

OSCAR (*Standing up*) Then let's play poker. (*Sharply, to the boys*) And watch your cigarettes, will you? This is my house, not a pig sty.

(*He takes the ashtray from the side table next to the armchair, bends down and begins to pick up the butts. The boys settle down to play poker*)

Curtain